The CARDIFF & SOUTH WALES Cook Book

A celebration of the amazing food & drink on our doorstep.
Featuring over 25 stunning recipes.

The Cardiff and South Wales Cook Book

©2018 Meze Publishing Ltd. All rights reserved.

First edition printed in 2018 in the UK.

ISBN: 978-1-910863-31-2

Thank you to: James Sommerin

Compiled by: Anna Tebble, Phil Turner, Will Savage

Written by: Katie Fisher, Muirne Cunning

Photography by: Jake Morley (www.jakemorley.co.uk)

Edited by: Phil Turner

Designed by: Matt Crowder, Paul Cocker

Contributors: Sarah Koriba, David Wilson, Alana Bishop, Rachel Havard, Jessica Findlow, Muirne Cunning, Zofia Filipowicz

Cover art: Luke Prest (www.lukeprest.com)

Published by Meze Publishing Limited
Unit 1b, 2 Kelham Square
Kelham Riverside
Sheffield S3 8SD
Web: www.mezepublishing.co.uk
Telephone: 0114 275 7709
Email: info@mezepublishing.co.uk
Printed by Bell and Bain Ltd, Glasgow

FOREWORD

Being born and bred in Wales, there was only one place I wanted to open my own restaurant. At the age of 16, I moved to Scotland and worked at Farleyer under the guidance of Richard Lyth. He taught me the understanding of seasonality, quality and the essence of flavour. I also achieved my first accolade here; Young Chef of the Year for Scotland.

I am not from a Michelin background so was overwhelmed when I achieved a Michelin star in 2007 at The Crown at Whitebrook and subsequently at my own restaurant in 2016. I think achieving it in Penarth was much more meaningful, as my family are here and to be the only Michelin-starred restaurant in the Cardiff area is amazing.

Restaurant James Sommerin is a family-run business; a big element of our ethos is family. My wife, Louise, works front of house and our eldest daughter Georgia works alongside her 'old man' in the kitchen. She quite often winds me up as her soufflés knock the socks off mine.

We also focus and pride ourselves on using local suppliers and locally sourced produce. Our fish is from a local fishmonger in Cardiff and our fruit, veg and meat are also Welsh and sourced as locally as possible. Supporting local suppliers and businesses is very important to me and the produce we have available in this part of the country is amazing.

Cardiff's food scene is definitely up and coming, with a diverse line-up of restaurants and cafés. You can find an array of different cuisines in the city including tapas, street food, bespoke cafés and bakeries. I love nothing more than taking the family out to a local tapas restaurant on a Monday evening when we're closed. I was delighted to be asked to be part of this special book celebrating all that this area, and my home, has to offer. I hope you enjoy it!

James Sommerin – Restaurant James Sommerin

CONTENTS

Fit for a KING

In rural Monmouthshire, 1861 Restaurant celebrates the bounty of the Welsh countryside by creating fine dining that's as unforgettably delicious as it is friendly and relaxed.

Simon and Kate King were working in a Monmouthshire hotel as head chef and wedding coordinator respectively when they met. Not long later Kate got to organise their own wedding, and then in 2007 they began another joint venture with the opening of 1861, a fine dining restaurant that aimed to pair excellent quality food with a relaxed and homely atmosphere. A friendly welcome – starting right from the table booking, which is always done over the phone so attention can be paid to the details, such as special requirements or celebrations, for each guest – is paramount, followed by a comfortable lunch or evening out for every visitor to the rural countryside location.

The menu reflects the lovely surroundings Simon and Kate's restaurant is set in; dishes are based on seasonal produce which is primarily sourced from small, independent suppliers across South Wales. As the recipes evolve from these natural pairings of fresh ingredients, the menu changes are ongoing with new dishes swapped in every day. The majority of fruit and vegetables used at 1861 are grown by Kate's dad, and local farmers form an important part of the network. This is also

true of the small team Simon and Kate employ to keep their service top-notch. "We're keen to train people in the industry we love," says Simon. Kate is the face of the restaurant; she knows many of their regular guests by name as they've seen plenty of returning diners over the years and her personable approach makes 1861 a pleasure to visit.

On entering the restaurant, Simon and Kate have created a lounge area for guests to have a drink and read through the menu without feeling rushed to decide; this is the first stage of a dining experience that's designed to welcome and put everyone at ease. With only around 10 tables in the dining room, it's an intimate setting to enjoy a seven course tasting menu or traditional yet refined à la carte dishes cooked with real care. Simon and Kate are very happily settled in the place and career they've built for themselves and their family, and are soon to turn 1861 into a restaurant with rooms as the next stage of their venture. "We consider ourselves very lucky to be in this area doing what we love."

Restaurant 1861

2018 MICHELIN

Restaurant 1861
ELDERFLOWER SOUFFLE

Soufflé has a reputation for being tricky to get right, but even if you don't get the most impressive rise at home, the delicate flavour of elderflowers in this recipe will come through for a beautiful end to a spring supper.

Preparation time: 15 minutes | Cooking time: approx. 30 minutes | Makes 8

Ingredients

For the soufflé base:

250g cooked apple purée

3 large umbels of elderflower

25g cornflour mixed with 2 tbsp cold water

For the soufflé:

250g egg whites

200g caster sugar

3 large umbels of elderflower

8 ramekins, brushed with melted butter and coated in sugar

Method

Preheat the oven to 180°c and pick all the elderflowers from the stalks into a bowl.

For the soufflé base

Carefully heat the apple purée and then add half the elderflowers (3 umbels worth). Mix through and then add the cornflour. Continue to cook until thickened. Remove from the heat and strain through a sieve into a large mixing bowl. Cover and keep warm.

For the soufflé

Whisk the egg whites to a soft peak using a table top mixer. Gradually add the caster sugar and continue to whisk until you have a stiff meringue. Place one large spoonful of the meringue into the soufflé base and mix thoroughly, then gently fold in the rest of the meringue a spoonful or two at a time until combined. Finally, add the remaining elderflowers and fold in gently to distribute throughout the mix. Spoon the mixture into ramekins and level the top off with a palette knife. Run the point of a knife around the top of the ramekin to release the edge of the mixture; this helps the rise. Bake in the preheated oven for 12-15 minutes until risen.

To serve

Serve immediately with your favourite accompaniment; I like a rhubarb sauce and sorbet.

Top tip

Use ovenproof coffee cups if you don't have ramekins; they are also easier to take out of the oven!

A world of GOODNESS

Hare Krishna monk and entrepreneur Adam El Tagoury set up Anna Loka – Cardiff's first completely vegan café – to inspire all food lovers by offering an eclectic and ethically conscious dining experience in Wales' diverse capital.

The key to understanding what Cardiff's first totally vegan café is all about is in its name: Anna Loka. In Sanskrit, the language of ancient India, 'anna' means food, health or earth, and 'loka' means world or planet. The combination of these two definitions effectively represents what the café offers; an eclectic, authentic, healthy experience that facilitates principled, conscious choices for food lovers (vegan or otherwise) without compromising on quality or taste.

At the heart of Anna Loka is Adam El Tagoury, a Hare Krishna monk, entrepreneur and passionate advocate for veganism, whose message he spreads through delicious food. Adam opened his unique café after seeing a need for a place where vegans could go and choose anything they fancied off the menu without worrying about the risk of cross contamination, while having an abundance of choice when dining out. Jan Taube joined the team as the head chef a year later, and is in charge of menu development. The wide range of options covers breakfast, lunch and dinner including hearty burgers, curries, a seasonal 'Krishna bowl', freshly made sweet treats and more refined dishes too – think turmeric buckwheat stuffed aubergine, charred Romanesco, kale crisps…

Jan is originally from Poland, and has been a vegan himself for just six months, but finds that inspiration flows from cuisines on every continent. From Middle Eastern spices to the comfort food of the American South, there is no part of the world that doesn't have something to offer. He really enjoys finding innovative ways of extracting flavour and texture from plant-based ingredients, using the natural world to experiment and invent new dishes.

The success of Anna Loka stems from all the passionate, committed people who work there. As the team themselves put it, "our restaurant can only prosper and provide opportunities for employment and growth when we continually improve ourselves, and the work we do." This ethos ties in with their commitment to the health of animals and the environment, with the ultimate aim of contributing to a kinder, more sustainable world in which people can enjoy delicious food and drink that benefits the planet too.

Anna Loka
ULTIMATE CASHEW AND BEETROOT BURGER

Our chef's tips: use ground spices if you do not have a grinder or a high speed blender, or just want to save time. You can swap out the French mustard for Dijon or English, but it will give the finished mayonnaise a sharper taste. Be careful not to overdo the garlic, as some types are much stronger than others, and avoid Chinese garlic as it contains a lot of pesticides.

Preparation time: 60 minutes | Cooking time: 15 minutes | Serves: 8

Ingredients

For the burger:

100g dry red lentils

150g cashew nuts

3 cloves of garlic

1-2 medium-sized red onions

12g yellow mustard seeds

8g cumin seeds

8g coriander seeds

12g fennel seeds

1 tbsp ground cardamom

2 green chillies

30g fresh ginger

20g fresh coriander

1 pack (250g) cooked baby beetroot

130g oats

2 tsp salt

1 tsp Demerara sugar

Oil for frying

For the garlic mayonnaise:

250ml unsweetened soy milk

3-4 cloves of garlic

1 tbsp French mustard

1½ tbsp white wine vinegar

½ tbsp lemon juice

1 tsp salt

½ tsp pepper

300ml rapeseed oil (preferably cold-pressed)

Method

For the burger

Firstly, place the lentils in a saucepan, cover with 300ml of fresh water and simmer for around 30 minutes, until they are tender and all the water has been absorbed (add more water during cooking if needed).

For the best results and quickest preparation, use a food processor for preparing the ingredients. Blitz the cashew nuts so they are roughly chopped. Transfer to a bowl and set aside. Finely chop the garlic in the food processor, then add the red onions and blend again. Toast the mustard seeds until they start popping, shaking the pan every 30 seconds to ensure they don't catch and burn. Toast the cumin, fennel and coriander seeds in the same way. Place all the spices in a grinder or clean food processor and blend until fine. Add the cardamom, chillies, ginger and fresh coriander and blend again.

Grate the beetroot into a large bowl. Keep the liquid and add all the prepared ingredients plus the oats, salt and sugar to the bowl. Mix well. If you feel the mixture is too wet and crumbly, add more oats (bear in mind that the chunkier the oats are, the more time it will take for them to absorb the water so try waiting 10 minutes and then check again). Form the burger mix into patties and fry them in batches, using a wide pan with just enough oil to cover the bottom.

For the garlic mayonnaise

Put all the ingredients apart from the oil into the clean food processor or into a bowl with a hand blender. Blend on high speed until the mixture has a smooth consistency (around 1 minute). Add the oil gradually while blending until the mayonnaise is nice and thick. You can add more oil for a thicker consistency.

Serving suggestion

To build the ultimate burger, you need: vegan garlic mayonnaise; sweet chilli sauce; beef tomatoes; romaine lettuce, gherkins; jalapeños and good bread buns.

Grill the burger buns, brushing a little oil on both sides first for a crispier texture. Cut the beef tomatoes into slices. Spread garlic mayonnaise over the bottom half of the bun and sweet chilli sauce over the top half. Place one lettuce leaf on the bottom, then a slice of beef tomato, two slices of gherkins and a few jalapeños. You can also use homemade slaw; mix it with a little bit of garlic mayo and mustard for extra crunch and flavour. Add one (or two!) patties to the stack and top with the bun, then get stuck in.

Gone FISHIN'

E. Ashton Fishmongers has been selling fish and game for over two hundred years in Cardiff, having passed down its success through generations of fishing families, and built up a reputation as one of the leading retailers for fish and game in the whole of the UK.

It's a rare business that can claim over two centuries of heritage, but E. Ashton Fishmongers is perfectly entitled to do just that. Having begun on Cardiff's high street in the year 1800, the fish and game seller was bought by an employee, Roger Ashton, in the 1870s and incorporated as a limited company by its namesake, Elizabeth Ashton, in the 1920s. This, along with the move to Cardiff Central market 30 years earlier where the business remains to this day, paved the way for generations of fishmongers to take the helm, from husband and wife to father and son.

When a family business has such longevity, there's always the temptation to keep things traditional. However, when John Adams – a fourth generation fishmonger himself, from Penarth – bought E. Ashton Fishmongers in 1973 he knew that the business needed to change and expand to keep up with the times. Today, under the direction of John's two sons, Jonathan and Nicholas, Ashton is still making waves in the world of quality fish and game retail, as well as fulfilling its role as part of Cardiff's culinary furniture.

Both John and his son Jonathan have been presidents of The National Federation of Fishmongers, and three of

Ashton's staff members have won the British Fish Craft Championship. Despite all these achievements though, Jonathan and Nicholas have kept the core values implemented by the very first owners at heart; they care deeply about their products, making sure their products are as tasty and fresh as possible, and take care to limit waste and buy sustainably wherever possible. With fish being bought and sold every day, it's often on ice in the store within 24 hours of being caught, an impressive achievement considering Ashton buys from 15 ports across the UK as well as importing directly from Rungis in Paris, the world's biggest international food market.

Ashton also specialises in French poultry and is Cardiff's largest game dealer, with top-quality classic options such as duck, free-range corn-fed chicken, guinea fowl, quail, and foie gras available thanks to buyer expertise. Nicholas and Jonathan have developed a range of exotic meats from ostrich to zebra alongside their traditional lines, showcasing their adventurous side which has brought the business so successfully into the 21st century. A pillar of the community, E. Ashton sees shoals of loyal customers returning year in, year out, and is looking forward to another 100 years in Cardiff!

ASHTON'S

1891
CARDIFF MARKET
MARCHNAD CAERDYDD

Ashton Fishmongers
LUXURY FISHERMAN'S PIE

This recipe is really simple but makes a deliciously comforting meal, especially in the winter. All the fish is interchangeable so you can alter the filling to suit your personal tastes, or you can always pick up a freshly prepared fish pie mix from our shop.

Preparation time: 15 minutes | Cooking time: approx. 1 hour | Serves: 4-6

Ingredients

75g butter

1 large onion, finely chopped

2 sticks of celery, finely chopped

1 leek, finely chopped

200g tinned sweetcorn, drained

100g frozen peas

200g Ashton's boneless salmon fillet

200g Ashton's boneless smoked haddock fillet

200g Ashton's boneless cod fillet

200g Ashton's peeled tiger prawns

40g plain flour

400ml whole milk

1 egg yolk

Salt and pepper

900g potatoes, boiled and mashed

Splash of milk

Handful of grated cheese (cheddar or similar)

Method

Preheat the oven to 190°c. Melt 25g of butter in a large frying pan and cook the onion, celery and leek until tender but not browned. Stir in the sweetcorn and peas and take the pan off the heat. Skin the fish fillets and cut into small pieces. Mix the fish and prawns into the cooked vegetable base and transfer everything into a 1.7 litre ovenproof dish.

Melt another 25g of butter in a saucepan and stir in the flour. Cook the paste gently for 1 minute, then remove from the heat and gradually stir in the milk. Return the pan to the heat when the milk has been fully incorporated, stirring constantly until the mixture thickens. Remove from the heat, add the egg yolk and season well.

Pour the white sauce over the pie filling. Add the remaining butter and enough milk to get a creamy consistency to the mashed potato. Pipe the potato on top to cover the filling completely. Bake the fish pie in the preheated oven for 30-35 minutes, adding a generous handful of grated cheese (sprinkled over the top) for the last 5 minutes of cooking time.

Hygge away FROM HOME

Brød is a Danish bakery and coffee shop run by Betina Skovbro, a Danish photographer turned baker who wanted to set the record straight when it came to her country's great pastry tradition...

Betina Skovbro, the owner and founder of Cardiff's first and only Danish bakery, began her journey fuelled by a desire to show the people of Wales how good a real Danish pastry could – and should be. With a background in photography, starting her own business was a new challenge, but the passion and emotional connection Betina has for baking has seen Brød go from strength to strength. She lived in Pontcanna then moved to the UK for work, so it felt like exactly the right place to set up, and Wales' capital city certainly agreed, having designated Brød the Best New Business and best Café/Coffee Shop in the Cardiff Life awards within two years of its opening!

The popular Danish bakery set out to "mash two traditions together" as Betina puts it – combining a take-away counter and a cosy coffee shop – to suit the local palate while introducing customers to the most authentic pastries, cakes and breads they'll find this side of the North Sea. Sitting down together to enjoy fresh coffee and pastries is part of a strong culinary tradition in Denmark and Brød recreates this by using the original Danish recipes with the best ingredients for its menu of sweet and savoury treats. Betina likes to source produce locally where she can, but also uses marzipan and malt for the rye bread – both far less common in the UK than across Scandinavia – from overseas.

The links to her home country, and to the provenance of her food and drink, are a big part of what makes Brød so unique. Betina's hard-working coffee shop team attend barista courses at the roasters who supply their coffee; her apprentice bakers have the opportunity to train in Denmark; and the team also visit their local suppliers, such as the mill that produces organic flour for the bakery. Betina grew up baking with her family, another mainstay of the Danish lifestyle, and even has her grandmother's reupholstered chairs, a collection of rolling pins including one of her great-grandmother's, and an oven purchased with money left to Betina by her grandmother surrounding her in the bakery and coffee shop.

The beautiful window displays open view into the bakery and a team who love what they create all encourage customers to embrace the Danish concept of hygge at Brød. There are plenty of regulars – families, couples, children and the postman who's partial to a good coffee! – to attest to the welcoming atmosphere Betina has created. The name of Betina's venture means bread, a nod to the homeliness and simplicity at the heart of her intentions for Brød and an invite to enjoy food and drink created with love.

Brød
DRØMME KAGE

The name of this recipe means 'Dream Cake' – a light but luxurious combination of a soft vanilla sponge with a caramelised coconut topping.

Preparation time: 10 minutes | Cooking time: approx. 45 minutes | Serves: 12-16

Ingredients

For the sponge:

225g caster sugar

3 eggs

75g softened butter

225g self-raising flour

2 tsp baking powder

150ml milk

½ tsp vanilla sugar

For the topping:

100g butter

150g desiccated coconut

250g dark brown sugar

75g milk

Pinch of salt

Method

For the sponge

Mix the sugar and butter with a whisk until combined before adding the rest of the ingredients and mix again until fully incorporated. The longer you stir a cake mixture, the denser and flatter the final result will be, so try to be efficient with your mixing and whisk for the minimum amount of time needed. Pour the mixture into a greased 22cm spring form cake tin, and bake for 35 minutes at 190°c.

For the topping

10 minutes before the sponge is done, start the coconut topping. Mix all the ingredients in a saucepan and stir over a medium heat until combined.

Make sure the sponge is fully cooked by checking the centre. It should spring back when pressed lightly, and a wooden skewer or thin knife poked into the sponge should come out clean. Smooth the topping and level it over the cake, then place it back into the oven to bake for another 5-8 minutes. Leave the cake to cool in the tin, and then serve.

Happy CAMPERS

From a converted camper van to a cosy cabin in one of Cardiff's busiest green spaces, the Brodie family has been on quite a journey...

Brodies Coffee Co began life as a mobile coffee shop, serving fresh coffee and home bakes at festivals and events across Wales. Husband and wife Ian and Danni were inspired by their travels around the world, particularly the coffee culture in Wellington, New Zealand, so on returning to the UK they converted a camper van and juggled full-time jobs with their new venture. The where, when and how of expanding and continuing the business, now with a baby boy on board, presented itself a few years later in the form of a listed cabin amidst Cardiff's Gorsedd Gardens. The derelict building, originally a park keeper's hut, underwent a full renovation and emerged a freshly painted, lantern-bedecked, fully fitted coffee shop in summer 2016.

Ian and Danni first linked up with the newly opened Coaltown Coffee Roasters when Brodies was just starting out, and the south west Wales roaster has supplied the young company ever since. Ian and Danni entrust the responsibility of providing customers with irresistible brownies, traybakes and cakes to local independent suppliers and by focusing on their two core values – great service and supporting other independents – they've proven that even in a very small space with limited equipment, it's possible to produce consistently great coffee, recognised by the Independent Coffee Guide for Wales and the South East, and sweet treats all year round.

The ethos that Ian and Danni stand by allows them to repay customers for supporting a small local company with fantastic produce that all feeds back into the local economy and community.

You can find the cabin itself by following strategically-placed signs throughout the park, designed to bring people to the door with a smile with quotes such as "a yawn is a silent scream for coffee". The park is a hotspot for seasonal events, family days out, student hang outs and working lunches, so it sees plenty of lively activity in all weathers. Being in a green space is very fitting for such an environmentally conscious business; Brodies uses compostable cups for all the take away drinks and eco-friendly packaging made by Vegware, a UK manufacturer.

With seating for around 20 people plus an outdoor space that's hard to beat, Brodies Coffee Co is drawing attention for all the right reasons in Cardiff. Ian and Danni hope to expand in the near future, bringing their perfect marriage of coffee and cake to a wider audience, and building on the recognition they are so proud to have achieved.

Brodies Coffee Co
EASY PEASY LEMON DRIZZLE CAKE

Crafted and perfected by Danni while baking for events with our coffee camper, this mega moist classic has always proven a hit. Whether at family fun days or the toughest triathlons, we've always found that the lemon drizzle has been our most popular creation. We find that this versatile beauty is best enjoyed with a cup of tea but is also a great accompaniment for an espresso!

Preparation time: 20 minutes | Cooking time: 40 minutes | Serves: 10

Ingredients

For the cake:

125g organic unsalted butter, softened

175g caster sugar

2 large free-range eggs

1 unwaxed lemon, zested

175g self-raising flour

Pinch of salt

4 tbsp whole milk

For the syrup:

1½ lemons, juiced

100g icing sugar

For the icing:

1 lemon, juiced

150g icing sugar

Method

Preheat the oven to 180°c and line a 2lb loaf tin with greaseproof paper or a ready-made loaf tin liner. In a mixing bowl, cream the butter and sugar, and then add the eggs and lemon zest. Beat everything together until the batter is nice and fluffy and then gently fold in the flour and salt. Add the milk and mix thoroughly.

Spoon the cake batter into the prepared tin and bake in the centre of the oven for 40 minutes (or until a skewer poked into the centre of the loaf comes out clean).

While the cake is baking, make the syrup to drizzle over the top. Gently heat the lemon juice and icing sugar in a saucepan until the sugar has dissolved. As soon as the cake comes out of the oven, poke holes all over the top with a skewer and pour over the syrup.

Now, be patient! Leave the cake to cool completely before removing it from the tin.

For the icing, combine the lemon juice and icing sugar until the mixture is smooth and white (add more icing sugar if needed). Drizzle the icing liberally all over the cake.

A friendly BUNCH

Combining sophisticated food and drink with a cosy Welsh welcome,
The Bunch of Grapes is committed to creativity and passion when it comes to
putting the gastro in gastropub.

On what is now a quiet backstreet in South Wales, The Bunch of Grapes can be found in a rather unlikely spot for an award-winning gastropub. The building itself dates back to 1851, when it served to slake the thirsts of workers from the nearby chainworks, Isambard Kingdom Brunel's 'Brown Lennox', alongside an old canal lock, a remnant of the once vital Glamorganshire Canal. The pub and the role it has played in Pontypridd is steeped in history, all of which can be read about at leisure in The Bunch's own illustrated history book.

It's the future that's at the forefront of The Bunch's aims these days though; the ever-evolving definition of 'gastropubs' and how to combine fine dining with great pub food. The pub has been in the Otley family since the 1980s, with Nick Otley at the helm since 2000, following his career as a fashion photographer. It was Nick's travels that inspired and transformed the culinary vision of The Bunch of Grapes, guiding it over time to become the CAMRA, Good Pub Guide and AA designated 'Pub of the Year' that it is today.

Since then, The Bunch has focused on its core ethos of using as much Welsh produce as possible, fostering relationships with local suppliers (even allotments sometimes) and very much moving with the seasons. There's even a garden on site where produce is grown, picked and transformed into garnishes for the menu that combines heritage and innovation from the small but tight-knit kitchen team who've worked together for many years now.

To wash it all down, The Bunch only stock from independent breweries and have been serving eight real ales, five craft kegs and real ciders for nearly 10 years (before it was trendy to go small-scale and local) as well as "a damn good wine list"! Beer festivals, meet-the-brewer events, themed cheese evenings, and cocktail nights complete the line-up at the relaxed venue that is passionate about great food, great drinks and great Welsh pubs.

BUN CHOF GRA PE S

May Lunch & Bar Menu

Mon - Thurs Lunch:
12pm - 3pm
Mon - Thurs Evening
4.30pm - 8.30pm
Fri & Sat:
12pm - 8.30pm

Starters

Fillet of Breconshire beef carpaccio, truf

Scorched fillet of mackerel, dill oil, poach

Heritage tomato bruschetta on charcoal

Pork, venison and juniper terrine, beer a

Devilled lambs' kidneys on toasted brea

Chargrilled Wye Valley asparagus, soft b

Mains

8oz / 10oz Breconshire beef sirloin stea
chips and peppercorn sauce £18.50 / £2

Pan fried pork loin chop in sage and bro
red wine onions & caramelised apple £1

Pan fried cod, crushed Jersey Royal new
butter £15.25

Smoked beetroot, tomato & pinto bean c
£13.80

Wild boar sausages with cider braised re

Bunch fish & chips with garden peas, hor

Homemade Campanelle pasta with field
& Hafod cheese shavings £11.75

Homemade Bunch beef burger with Buffa
and Pwll Mawr mature cheddar with han

The Bunch of Grapes

WILD GARLIC GNOCCHI WITH TENDERSTEM BROCCOLI AND WILD GARLIC PESTO

A fresh, vibrant and seasonal take on gnocchi. The dish showcases how cheap and delicious ingredients treated simply can serve up flavour alongside elegance and nutrition. Its popularity at The Bunch has spearheaded the evolution of our meat-free dishes.

Preparation: 15-20 minutes | Cooking: 3 hours | Serves: 4

Ingredients

For the gnocchi:

700g baking potatoes (allow 100g loss for skins)

Salt and olive oil

125g '00' grade pasta flour

100g wild garlic, chopped

2 tsp salt

For the pesto:

100g almonds

120g wild garlic

1 large handful of parsley

150ml olive oil

To finish:

100g morel mushrooms

100g garden peas

100g edamame beans

1 bunch of spring onions, chopped

200g tenderstem broccoli

Method

For the gnocchi

Preheat the oven to 200°c. Wrap the potatoes in foil with a pinch of salt and a drizzle of olive oil. Place on a baking tray and bake for at least an hour, or until soft. Once cooked, scoop the flesh out of the skins and leave to cool. Combine the flour, wild garlic and salt and then mix this into the potato with a spoon until smooth (lumps are not good for gnocchi!).

Lay your cling film on a clean work surface. Shape the mix into logs and then wrap in cling film. Roll tightly to achieve an even width along the log, making sure there is no air in the cling film (if you need to release air make a small hole in the cling film and re-wrap). Tie the ends of the logs off tightly.

Place the logs into simmering water and cover. Leave to simmer for 40 minutes. Remove the logs from the water and allow to cool. Once cooled, place in the fridge for an hour to chill. Remove the cling film and then cut the gnocchi into slices approximately 1cm thick.

For the pesto

Add all ingredients to a blender and blitz.

To finish

Sauté the morel mushrooms, peas, edamame beans and spring onions lightly. Add the tenderstem broccoli with a small splash of water and simmer for three minutes until cooked. Meanwhile, lightly flour the gnocchi and place in a hot frying pan, turning once golden brown.

To serve

Spoon the pea and bean mix into the centre of the plate. Arrange the broccoli around the peas and arrange the gnocchi around the side of the greens as shown. To finish, garnish with pesto to personal taste.

Formulating the
PERFECT PATTY

Vision and fresh produce is at the forefront of Burger Theory's ethos, bringing only the best beef to your table.

The burger boys, owners and friends Rory Perriment, Nicolas Makin and Oliver Thorogood, dub themselves as the 'creative burger people' because what sets Burger Theory apart from the rest is its commitment to creativity, drawing inspiration from cuisines across the globe. They focus solely on burgers because they love that they're essentially a whole meal in a bun. "There are so many flavours out in the world, and we wanted to make the most of it," Rory says.

Founder Rory initially worked as a chef before opening Burger Theory and is largely self-taught. He set up Burger Theory six years ago, aged 24, becoming part of the street food scene, soon progressing to festivals and always developing and playing around with recipes. His enthusiasm for great food led Burger Theory to residencies in various pop-ups before establishing the first Burger Theory restaurant in Bristol in August 2017.

Wanting to expand, Rory chose Cardiff as the perfect place to establish a permanent base and make it his second restaurant after Bristol, because of the strong regional cuisine and the extensive local produce available. Burger Theory has resided in Kongs Bar since 2016 but now have an exciting new project underway. In 2018 the business opens the doors to its very own Cardiff restaurant, designed for casual dining in a comfortable space filled with art, which reflects the creativity in every aspect of Burger Theory. Presentation is something the team pride themselves on, producing the picture perfect burger time and time again with minute attention to detail.

"We very much do everything our own way," says Rory. The kitchen team make their own sauces and burgers from scratch, source their beef from one farm through one butcher and use only free-range poultry. The menu isn't completely carnivorous though; a quarter of the offerings accommodate Burger Theory's many vegetarian and vegan customers who, with 16 burgers to choose from, are regular visitors.

The crew's hard work and enthusiasm make Burger Theory an incredibly popular eatery all round. The table service is friendly, and there's a great craft beer list plus plenty of cocktails to tickle all taste buds. As part of Cardiff's innovative and expanding food and drink scene, and with Cardiff's very own Burger Theory restaurant on its way, these creative burger people are here to stay. Expect this burger team to continue bringing flavours from all over the world together with flair and fun.

Burger Theory

THE KIMCHEESE BURGER /KIMCHI AND BEEF SHORT RIB NOODLE STIR-FRY

The Kimcheese Burger has become a firm favourite at Burger Theory. We love the idea that anything can be made into a burger, even Korean food. Kimchi is one of Korea's biggest flavours and incredibly good for you. Here we have given you a burger recipe that can also be made into a noodle stir-fry. Enjoy!

Preparation time: 1 hour | Cooking time: 7 hours | Serves: 6

Ingredients

For the beef short rib:

2kg beef short ribs

Salt and pepper

570ml (1 pint) light ale

125ml white wine vinegar

80g Demerara sugar

For the black pepper sauce:

50g salted butter

500ml cooking liquid from beef pan

2 cloves of garlic, crushed

5g black peppercorns, crushed

120ml light soy sauce

80g sugar

For the burgers:

1kg ground beef (20% fat)

3g ground black pepper

Grated cheddar cheese

Sea salt, to taste

6 burger buns

Mayo, lettuce, sliced tomato and sliced red onion

Turn it into stir-fry!

Your favourite noodles

To garnish either dish:

Kimchi (available at health food shops and Asian supermarkets)

Sliced spring onions, chillies and chopped salted peanuts

Method

For the beef short rib

Preheat the oven to 200°c. Place the ribs in a snug fitting roasting tray and season with salt and pepper. Pour the beer and vinegar over the ribs and sprinkle the sugar on. Fill the tray with water until the ribs are covered. Cover with tin foil and cook for 5-6 hours, until the meat is falling off the bone. Save the cooking liquid for the black pepper sauce. Pull the beef off the bone, removing most of the fat.

For the black pepper sauce

Add all of the ingredients to a saucepan. Simmer until reduced by three quarters. Strain the sauce through a sieve. Stir through the beef rib meat.

For the burgers

Mix the beef with the black pepper and mould into six patties. Season the outside with sea salt. Toast the buns. In a pan on a medium heat, cook the patties for 3 minutes on one side, flip them over and place the cheese on top straight away to melt it. Cook for another 3 minutes. Allow to rest on a plate for one minute. In another pan heat the pulled beef on a low heat. Dress the bun with mayo, lettuce, tomato and red onion. When everything is ready assemble the burger in this order: beef patty, followed by pulled beef and finally the kimchi. Garnish with spring onions, fresh chillies and peanuts.

Turn it into stir-fry!

Cook your favourite noodles according to the instructions on the packet. In a wok, fry the kimchi on a medium-high heat in a little oil. Add the noodles and pulled beef to the pan and heat through. Garnish with spring onions, fresh chillies and peanuts.

A match made
IN BODLON

Nia and Colin played to their individual strengths to create a café and gift shop that perfectly pairs traditional dishes with Welsh gifts and hampers.

Nia Evans' successful online business – specialising in gifts and hampers of Welsh products – transformed when she joined forces with her partner, Welsh chef Colin Gray, to open Caffi Bodlon in the leafy Cardiff suburb of Whitchurch. Combining their areas of expertise resulted in a café and gift shop where freshly cooked food, a tempting deli section and exclusive arty gifts celebrate the best of Welsh good taste. This homely approach has been met with great approval by the locals and has earned Nia and Colin's venture a 'must visit' reputation.

The food that Colin creates for Caffi Bodlon very much reflects his love of Wales and the rich vein of food and drink he can tap into. Traditional but still hugely popular fare like lamb cawl, and Welsh rarebit of course, sit amongst a range of lunch and breakfast options. Homemade cakes and pastries hit the spot for a post-shopping treat, especially paired up with a fresh coffee or cup of tea. Word has travelled about the fantastic quality of the seasonally-influenced menus, which means that bagging a table (especially on a Friday lunchtime) can be quite a feat!

Bodlon also boasts a deli section, where customers can enjoy choosing even more Welsh specialities and old favourites to enjoy back home. From gin to chocolate, the array of tasty treats is sourced from Wales and complemented by the selection of gifts chosen by Nia. Many of these are designed exclusively for Bodlon and the collection includes ceramics, jewellery, slate, textiles, cards and prints, to name a few. With so much to choose from, it seemed that people just couldn't get enough of the café and gift shop during its daytime hours. So, Nia and Colin started to host monthly evening events at Bodlon – filled with live music and accompanied by posh pizza, Welsh tapas, wine tastings and more – that quickly became oversubscribed and are always thoroughly enjoyed.

The enterprising couple opened a second gift shop shortly after their first venue took off and have even more exciting developments ahead of them. Construction of the new Cegin Bodlon (Bodlon Kitchen) has already begun, expanding on the deli side of the business and including a hot food bar, more unusual and unmissable products, allotment produce and Wales's first nut grinding machine to make fresh nut butter! From a perfect pair to a terrific trio, Nia and Colin know just how to match the best with the best.

Caffi Bodlon
WELSH RAREBIT

This is one of the most popular dishes on the menu at Caffi Bodlon; a traditional Welsh dish using Colliers mature cheddar and Gower Gold real ale, made on the Gower near Swansea. Delicious served with crispy bacon and spiced pear chutney like we do.

Preparation time: 15 minutes | Cooking time: 10 minutes | Makes: 500g (enough for 10-15 pieces of toast)

Ingredients

225ml Welsh ale (not dark, but not too light either – Gower Gold is our choice)

340g mature Welsh cheddar (Colliers extra-mature is best)

40g Welsh salted butter

15ml Worcestershire sauce

15g Dijon or English mustard

30g plain flour

Method

Bring the beer to the boil in a heavy-based, preferably non-stick saucepan. Reduce until you have about half the amount you started with (around 110ml – it's important to measure this as it affects the flavour and consistency of the mix). Grate the cheese and then add all the remaining ingredients to the saucepan. Stir with a wooden spoon or spatula until the cheese melts and the mixture starts to bubble slightly. It will thicken and should be shiny with no lumps. Use a whisk to get a smooth mixture if needed.

At this point you can transfer the rarebit mixture into an airtight container, leave it to cool and then store it in the refrigerator for up to 10 days. It can also be frozen.

Toast some thickly cut sourdough on one side only. Turn over and spread the rarebit mixture thickly on the untoasted side, pushing it right up to the edges. Place under a hot grill and heat until golden brown and bubbling. Allow to cool for a minute or so before attempting to cut, and then serve immediately with grilled bacon, your favourite spicy or fruity chutney and a green salad on the side.

Canna get more WELSH

Canna Deli offers a unique and authentic range of Welsh produce, from handmade cheese to boutique chutneys and you simply can't leave without a little slice of home.

Armed with her artisan cheese, made on her family's dairy farm, Elin left her job as a science teacher and opened Canna Deli in 2015. Tucked between KITI, a ladies boutique, and Barney & Beau, a children's boutique, this hidden gem has wowed its customers since the very beginning. With all Welsh-speaking staff and ingredients exclusively sourced in Wales, Elin really knows how to create a traditional Welsh experience.

The family's artisan cheese is the star of the show of course, being award-winning and handcrafted in Anglesey. Canna Deli stocks a wide range of delicious varieties to choose from, and if great cheese just isn't enough, then you can also find plenty of enticing local products to complement it. From cured meats and charcuterie, to wines and ciders from Snowdonia, Canna Deli will take you on a tour of Wales without leaving the front door!

Elin has put together such a treasure trove that as well as feasting your eyes at Canna Deli you can feast for real from the café's extensive menu. With a seasonal specials board, a very popular brunch menu and traditional Welsh dishes to choose from, there's plenty to try before you buy, all homemade with Welsh ingredients of course. Canna Deli is also fully licensed so you can easily swap your award-winning coffee for a local beer or glass of wine and even enjoy it outdoors while relaxing in the sunshine – if you're lucky! – making the café a great setting for a long lunch or a chilled afternoon after browsing the deli shelves.

Sunday lunching and artisan food shopping are complimented by a busy events calendar at Canna Deli. Elin holds monthly evening events, such as tapas nights and gin tastings, and also takes bookings for birthdays and parties. These often draw in new customers looking for something a bit different yet still close to home, and the café and deli are havens for regulars who love the variety and quality to be found there. Elin's approach to her unique venture has proved popular across the board; being able to find the best of Welsh produce under one roof is a real celebration of Wales and its culinary class.

Canna Deli
BRIXTON BRUNCH

Perfect for relaxed Sunday mornings, this brunch is easy to put together but looks so pretty on the plate. More importantly, it tastes great!

Preparation time: 20 minutes | Cooking time: 10 minutes | Serves: 2

Ingredients

2 thick slices of Pettigrew Bakery sourdough

1 pack of halloumi, sliced

2 fresh free-range eggs

2 avocados

Small bunch of coriander, chopped

Salt and pepper

Drizzle of Blodyn Aur rapeseed oil

Knob of Shirgar salted butter

A few chives, finely chopped

A few edible flowers

Method

Begin by placing the sourdough under the grill to toast. Meanwhile, lightly fry the halloumi over a medium-high heat for 2 minutes each side, or until golden brown in colour.

Gently crack the first egg into a small cup. In a pan of simmering seasoned water, create a vortex by swirling a spoon around, drop the egg in the centre and then poach for 3-4 minutes depending on how runny you like your yolk. Do the same with the other egg.

Mash the avocado flesh in a bowl and mix in the chopped coriander, salt, pepper and a drizzle of Blodyn Aur rapeseed oil.

Butter the toast, scoop a good dollop of avocado mixture on top, place the grilled halloumi on the avocado, then lay the poached egg on top.

To serve

To garnish the beautiful brunch, sprinkle over some chopped chives and some edible flowers. Sprinkle with a little salt and pepper to taste if you like, and enjoy!

One stop SHOP

Cardiff Market's long history of friendly traders and local produce continues alongside the innovation and diversity that characterises its incredible range of stalls and produce today.

Shopping local by visiting dedicated independent retailers was the way it always used to be and luckily for Cardiff residents it's still possible to do just that in the vibrant city centre. Owned and operated by Cardiff Council, Cardiff Market is a haven for the best local traders and a treasure trove where you can buy almost anything under one soaring glass roof. Its 100% occupancy across over 240 permanent stalls does more than hint at how popular this destination continues to be from both sides of the till! No wonder, when you can buy anything from fresh fruit to nuts and bolts, and stop along the way for a cup of tea or a plateful of international street food; as market manager Louise Thomas says, "you name it, it's in there!"

Cardiff Market has been the place to go for shopping under one roof (literally) since 1891, when the covered market that exists today opened, though the team believe that there has been a market on that same site dating back to the 14th century. The council are in the process of putting together an archive detailing all their finds on this incredible heritage, but for those who prefer their history living, all it takes is a stroll around the beautiful Victorian structure. The Grade II* listed building consists of a ground floor and a balcony that wraps around the interior walls, and displays all its original features such as the wood panelling and, of course, many of the stalls themselves.

Longevity isn't only the preserve of the building, though, as several businesses can lay claim to decades of trading at the market. E. Ashton Fishmongers are a family business (also featured in this book) who date their own history as a seller of fresh fish and seafood back to the 1860s at the Trinity Street entrance to the market. Another family business, The Market Deli, have held the same stall since 1928 where five generations have presided over a range of food and drink products. There are photographs, too, of a Marks and Spencer original 'Penny Bazaar' stall – one of the first in the country, according to the council's research – which opened around 1895 alongside the butchers, bakers and skilled makers of Cardiff.

That range is still very much in evidence today, with a collection of goods for sale that leaves no customer behind. Top quality meat, game, fish, and seafood vie for attention next to boxes of colourful fruit and vegetables. The aroma of fresh bakes – from bread to Welsh cakes – is hard to resist, as is the promise of a restorative hot drink in one of several cosy coffee shops. There are plenty of traders who specialise in particular goods, such as cheese, spices, vegetarian and vegan fare, so every base is covered when it comes to your weekly shop or lunch on the hoof. It's not just about edibles, though, as those in the market for fabrics, pet supplies, cookware, electrical goods, flowers, music, gifts of all kinds and more won't be disappointed.

Louise and her team actively encourage the diversification of Cardiff Market because they are keen for it to represent and provide for the community as a whole. "We see people who come in every day for tea and toast," says Louise, "and so there are lots of customers that we know very well – the traders are familiar faces for them." The council also employ market porters to assist shoppers, making sure everyone gets a friendly welcome and, whether it's a first or a hundredth visit, can enjoy the experience. Part of the market's future plans involve a restoration of the interiors – including painting in the original colours that will be unearthed during clean ups – and bringing generations together in the ever-evolving space.

Cardiff Market already works with up-and-coming independent businesses, as well as supporting its long-standing traders, to bring the best of the city's food and drink scene to the attention of its residents and many visitors. Owners of independent restaurants whose premises are further out of the city can create a base that's easily accessible and a great step up for small businesses starting out, allowing them to gather a following and enjoy the draw of the market that brings a range of customers to their offering. "We'd also love to look at creating an events space within the market," says Louise. As a hub of food and drink in the city, Cardiff Market is not to be missed, and as a place to do a spot of shopping it certainly beats the supermarkets as a celebration of all things Cardiff!

COFFEE

HARD LINES

COFFEE
OTHER STUFF
HOUSE
REGION ALVAR

PRESSO 2.2
TEA 2.0
PROCESS WAS
G BLACK 2.4
HOT CHOCOLATE 2.8
TASTING NOTE
TADO 2.6
CHAI LATTE 2.8
WHITE 2.6
BARBARA
GUEST K
TE / CAPPUCCINO 2.6
SOFT DRINKS AVAILABLE
CH BREW 2.4
SEASONAL

If the CHOUX FITS...

Laurian Veaudour pursued the dream he'd had since childhood to set up his own modern patisserie, where he now creates delicate pastries, cakes, macarons and more to share with and inspire others.

Pâtissier Laurian Veaudour had called Cardiff home for almost a decade when he seized the opportunity to open his own patisserie in the city. His ethos of sticking to the goals you want to achieve and discovering what suits you, rather than trying to please everyone, has resulted in a steadily growing business, and although Cocorico Patisserie has won several awards in its time, the customers who return again and again are the real measure of this success for Laurian.

Cocorico is modern, creative and driven by passionate people who aim to provide something special and different, whether for a weekend lunch or a wedding. Laurian and his two experienced pastry chefs, who also trained in France, create sweet patisserie treats in the kitchen every day. The eye-catching display counter usually includes twelve different types of cake, chocolate bonbons, traditional French delicacies with beautiful finishes and macarons in all colours and flavours. They also offer lots of options for bespoke creations to suit individual occasions, ranging from celebration cakes to classic entremets and croquembouche.

Despite the French context of the venture, when it comes to ingredients – and indeed to national identities – there are no hard and fast rules at Cocorico. Laurian considers himself half-Welsh and chooses his suppliers and staff depending on what's most suited to his style of patisserie and cooking rather than what might be classified as the best, as well as sourcing locally wherever possible. He's keen on the concept of self-sufficiency too, and already cures his own bacon and bakes sourdough bread at the cafe, which is used in the menus of freshly made breakfasts, lunches and afternoon teas available throughout the day.

Already host to regular pop-ups and events, Cocorico Patisserie now also offers cookery classes for those wanting to make their cake and eat it! Laurian teaches the monthly full-day introduction to patisserie himself, which provides its students with the know-how to create six different cakes (as well as lunch and more treats to take home). He wanted to set up the school because sharing skills and inspiring a younger generation is something he enjoys and hopes to do more of, having discovered that challenging yourself, meeting new people, and learning from others are the key ingredients for making a dream come true.

Cocorico Patisserie

COCORICO
PATISSERIE

Cocorico Patisserie
TARTE AU CHOCOLAT

This is one of my all-time favourites. Simple recipes are often the best and you never can go wrong with a good chocolate treat.

Preparation time: 15 minutes, plus 1 hour minimum chilling time | Cooking time: 30 minutes
Makes 12 small or 1 large tarte

Ingredients

For the sweet pastry:

250g plain flour

125g icing sugar

125g unsalted butter, cubed

55g egg yolk

For the salted caramel:

60g UHT whipping cream

½ vanilla pod

65g unsalted butter, cubed

150g caster sugar

4g sea salt flakes

For the chocolate ganache:

375g UHT whipping cream

275g dark chocolate (70% cocoa solids)

75g unsalted butter, cubed

Method

For the sweet pastry

Blend the plain flour, icing sugar and unsalted butter in a food processor until you get a sandy texture. Add the egg yolk and mix well until all the ingredients come together.

Leave for 1 hour or even better, overnight in the fridge. Roll out to the pastry to 3-5mm thickness. Lay the rolled out dough in a tart case and gently mould it into the sides and base. Bake the pastry case in the oven at 150°c for 15-20 minutes. The case needs to cool before being filled.

For the salted caramel

Warm the whipping cream, vanilla pod and butter together in a small saucepan and then remove the vanilla pod. In another saucepan, heat 50g of the sugar then add the rest a bit at a time and keep on stirring until the sugar turns into a golden brown caramel. Add the cream mixture to the caramel along with the salt and mix until the caramel is fully dissolved. Use the mixture quickly as it will harden when cool.

For the ganache

Break the chocolate into small pieces and place in a heatproof bowl. Bring the cream to the boil and then pour it over the chocolate. Add the butter and blend using a stick blender to create a chocolate emulsion. This is now ready to use straight away.

To assemble

Pour the caramel in to the tart case to form a distinct layer, and then fill the case up with ganache. Leave to set room temperature for 2 hours for best results, and then serve and enjoy!

Cocorico Patisserie
TARTE AU CITRON

This is a classic that will always be on trend, but if you feel like jazzing it up,
why not swap the lemon juice for grapefruit juice and add a little splash of gin!

Preparation time: 30 minutes, plus 1 hour minimum chilling time | Cooking time: 30-60 minutes
Makes 12 small or 1 large tarte

Ingredients

For the sweet pastry:

250g plain flour

125g icing sugar

125g unsalted butter, cubed

55g egg yolk

For the lemon curd:

4 eggs

300g caster sugar

40g cornflour

200ml lemon juice

225g unsalted butter, cubed

For the Italian meringue:

200g caster sugar

50ml water

100g egg white

Method

For the sweet pastry

Blend the plain flour, icing sugar and unsalted butter in a food processor until you get a sandy texture. Add the egg yolk and mix well until the all the ingredients come together

Leave for 1 hour or overnight in the fridge. Roll out the pastry to 3-5mm thickness. Lay the rolled out dough in a tart case and gently mould it into the sides and base. Bake the pastry case in the oven at 150°c for 15-20 minutes. The case needs to cool before being filled.

For the lemon curd

Mix eggs and sugar together. Mix the cornflour and lemon juice together and then combine with the egg mixture. You can either cook the curd in a microwave for about 10 minutes on full power, stopping every 1½ minutes to stir, or cook it in a bain-marie for around 45 minutes stirring periodically. Once the mixture is the right consistency, add the butter while the mixture is still hot. Cover with cling film (to prevent a skin forming) and set aside.

For the Italian meringue

Mix the caster sugar and water together and cook in a pan until the temperature of the mixture reaches 121°c. Place the egg whites in a clean electric mixer bowl with a whisk attachment. Turn the mixer on and pour the sugar syrup onto the egg whites in a steady stream. Turn the mixer up to full speed and whisk until the meringue mixture is glossy and has lots of volume. Slow the mixer down to medium speed, and then turn it off once the mixture has cooled. Transfer the meringue into a piping bag.

To assemble

Fill the tart case with the curd – both should be cooled – and then finish the tart with the meringue. Pipe in swirls or lines as desired and then scorch the top with a blowtorch to get a lovely golden brown finish.

The perfect CURE

Curado Bar is a fusion of urban style and Spanish tastes, incorporating space to hang out and enjoy great food and drink as well as a deli that's floor-to ceiling with delicious and authentic products.

Shumana and Paul already had a wealth of experience in providing people with authentic Spanish experiences when they decided to open Curado Bar, but wanted to take their specialism even further with their newest venture. The husband and wife team own Ultracomida, a company that searches Spain for the best of its food and drink, imports directly from small producers to the UK and sells a fantastic range of products online and wholesale. There are already two existing restaurant-delis in Aberystwyth and Narberth under the Ultracomida umbrella, but Curado Bar has taken a step away from its sister company and aims to diversify the offering of Spanish food in the city.

Expanding into Cardiff was a long-held ambition for Shumana and Paul, so when they finally found the perfect space, opposite the stadium in the heart of the city, it was important to let both elements of Curado Bar shine through on their own merit. In other words, you won't find any stereotypical features that announce Curado's Spanish-ness: the clean industrial interior lets the food and drink speak for itself and vice versa! This approach has introduced a host of locals and visitors to the lesser known delights of Northern Spanish food and drink that makes up the Curado menu, such as over 25 Spanish wines by the glass, gins from Spanish distilleries, speciality meats and cheese, para picar (bar snacks) and pintxos (beautifully prepared finger food).

Anything you can taste at the bar can be bought in the deli; it's the ultimate try before you buy (if the hams hanging from the ceilings, wall of wines and open shelves packed with colourful products aren't enough to tempt) and much more fun than shopping in the supermarket! Curado also puts on regular events for producers to showcase their wares, where food lovers or budding wine connoisseurs can have a taste and learn about how the product is made from the makers themselves. Supplier relationships are one of the company's strengths, stemming from Ultracomida's years of successful operation but also from Paul's Valencian roots. The house beer at Curado Bar was created especially by a company in Valencia, whose owners Shumana and Paul met on holiday and now enjoy a productive partnership with – a perfect analogy for what Curado offers Cardiff: a balanced fusion between the urban and the unusual.

Curado Bar
CARPACCIO DE BACALAO AHUMADO

On one of Paul's buying trips to Spain he came across this dish in Valencia and fell in love with its simplicity and elegance. Spanish food is a way of life and a way of connecting with friends and family, so it's about using great ingredients, big flavours, and leaving yourself time to enjoy the company as well as the meal. If you can't find smoked salt cod you can substitute with super fresh raw cod, thinly sliced.

Preparation time: 15 minutes | Serves: 1

Ingredients

70-80g smoked salt cod, thinly sliced and coated in oil

20g tomato, peeled and grated

10g black olive paste (we use the "Ferrer" brand)

20 capers

25g Hualdo picual olive oil (or any good quality extra-virgin olive oil, preferably fruity rather than peppery)

Pinch of ground black pepper

Method

Spread the pieces of bacalao (salt cod) onto a plate so that the plate is covered with a thin layer of the fish. Dot the plate with the grated tomato, and the black olive paste. Lastly, scatter on the capers and drizzle with olive oil, before finishing with some black pepper to taste.

To serve
Pour yourself a glass of Galician white wine and grab a fork!

Applauding APPETITE

At Cardiff's home for the performing arts, Marc Corfield's charitable dining at Ffresh takes centre stage.

First opened in 2004, Wales Millennium Centre has since inspired millions of Cardiff Bay visitors with the best creative work from all over the world and its own stage productions that celebrate local talent. A food offering has been there from the beginning, but it wasn't until a decade later that the new head chef Marc Corfield decided to change the way it operates and make a fresh start.

The restaurant and bar work with the other elements of the WMC to give back to the Cardiff Bay community. The centre is a registered charity, where every penny is reinvested into charitable work and food is often inspired by stage productions. Various collaborations with local producers are used to mark milestones, such as special edition ale brewed in celebration of the world premiere of WMC's own musical. As the name implies, Ffresh always casts local, seasonal produce as the leading role in it's kitchen. "The alternating menus revolve around showcasing Welsh goods with an emphasis on tradition," says Marc. Working with familiar recipes such as smoked haddock chowder or apple crumble, but raising the game with different textures and modern presentation has earned Ffresh plenty of local accolades including Highly Recommended at the Food Awards Wales 2018.

The restaurant combines relaxed dining with world class entertainment, offering the guests an experience that satiates both body and mind. Catering to those wanting a quick pre-matinee bite as well as more leisurely eaters, the spacious venue works around different needs. Cosily lit at night and decorated with gleaming copper trees, it nods to the Welsh landscape and stage scenography, creating an enchanted forest fairytale atmosphere anyone can unwind in.

"We're family-friendly and accessible to all. We really want people to feel at home here," adds Marc, which is further reflected by the interiors. The exposed dining section provides plenty of space and light from the surrounding window walls, whereas more secluded booths will be appropriate for couples or cocktail drinkers looking for a little intimacy; on certain evenings they'll be accompanied by live music, comedy or musical theatre.

Ffresh has grown to play an important part in the Millennium Centre's infrastructure, echoing its pride in all things Welsh, unique and independent. With provenance of produce at its core, Marc's food ensures the pre-show doesn't fall short from what's yet behind the curtain, and for that a standing ovation is in order.

Fresh
FILLET OF COD WITH LAVERBREAD AND SPICED MUSSEL BROTH

This dish combines some of the best Welsh ingredients: mussels, samphire (also known as sea asparagus) and laverbread (the cooked form of laver seaweed). The sauce recipe stems from French cuisine and is a form of 'mouclade' – a traditional sauce with a hint of curry spice that is often paired with mussels – which gives a satisfying finish to the entire dish.

Preparation time: 20 minutes | Cooking time: 35 minutes | Serves: 4

Ingredients

For the crusted cod fillets:

800g cod fillet, skinned

100g breadcrumbs or some stale bread rolls

150g butter, unsalted

60g laverbread

1 lemon, zested

Pinch of salt and pepper

For the mussel broth:

500g mussels (we use Welsh mussels from Ashton Fishmonger in Cardiff Market)

100g Puy lentils

500g small new potatoes

125ml dry white wine

100ml sunflower or vegetable oil

80g shallots, finely chopped

50g garlic, finely chopped

50g ginger, grated

20g biryani paste

2g ground cumin

1 saffron thread (if not available, a pinch of saffron powder would work too)

1 lemon, juiced

100g crème fraiche

50ml olive oil

15g sea salt

Pinch of black pepper

1kg leeks, chopped

150g samphire

Method

Preheat the oven to 180°c.

For the crusted cod fillets

If using, grate the rolls into breadcrumbs. Melt the butter and pour it into a mixing bowl or a food processor. Add the breadcrumbs, laverbread, lemon zest, and a pinch of salt and pepper, and mix until combined. Portion the cod and spread the breadcrumb mix as evenly as possible over the cod fillets. Place on a baking tray.

For the mussel broth

Wash and scrub the mussels and remove the beards. Put to one side.

Wash the lentils, then place in a pan and bring to the boil. Once they start to boil, discard the liquid through a sieve and once again cover the lentils with fresh water and cook until soft. Then strain again to discard the water.

Place the potatoes in a pan with salted water, then bring to the boil and simmer until cooked. Heat another large saucepan, add the mussels to the pan with the white wine and cover with the lid. Steam the mussels until they are mostly open, remove them and set to one side. Strain the mussel liquid, allowing time for any grit to settle at the bottom, and set to one side.

Heat another heavy-based pan, then add the oil to fry off the shallots, garlic, and ginger until softened. Add the biryani paste, cumin, saffron, lentils and mussel juice, then cook gently for 10 minutes. While this is cooking, place the crusted cod fillets in the oven (allow 12 minutes approximately for this).

Once the sauce is cooked, blend in a liquidiser or with a hand blender. Add the lemon juice, crème fraîche, olive oil and seasoning, then blitz again until smooth. Place the finished sauce back into the pan, then add the new potatoes. In a separate pan, bring some salted water to the boil (enough to completely cover the leeks and samphire) and then add the leeks. Cook for one minute and then add the samphire. Once these are cooked, strain through a sieve, add to the pan with the potatoes and sauce. Stir to coat the potatoes and vegetables with sauce.

To serve

Divide this between four large bowls, then place the portions of cooked cod in the centre of each bowl and serve.

Fantastic Mr and MRS FOXY

Mr Foxy wanted to set up a deli, and Mrs Foxy wanted to move back to Wales – the creation of Foxy's Deli and Café in Penarth proved a perfect compromise and a hit with the locals.

Having decided to turn their individual dreams into a shared reality, Sian and Neil left London in 2002 to put down new roots in the characterful town of Penarth. The move combined a welcome return to Wales for Sian, and the fulfilment of Neil's ambition to set up a deli full of fantastic food and fresh produce. Foxy's Deli and Café has since established itself as a real hub of the community and is flourishing amongst the independent businesses and people in the area who love to create and enjoy local fare.

Good food and drink is the name of the game at Foxy's, from organic honey to an all-Welsh afternoon tea complete with Bara Brith and the eponymous cakes. Sian and Neil have adapted their venture to suit the tastes and demands they have encountered over the years, leading to a veritable Aladdin's cave that now offers both visitors and locals a unique selection of Welsh delights. They stock the full range of Nom Nom chocolate bar – featuring unusual flavours made with passion and outside-the-box thinking in West Wales – lots of Pen Y Lan preserves, Snowdonia cheeses, artisan honey from traditional beekeeper Coedcanlas and much more, not to mention their very own Foxy's ale, made for them by three-man microbrewery Tomos a Lilford.

Sourcing produce from and supporting these very individual set ups has resulted in Foxy's Deli being listed amongst Rick Stein's food heroes, as well as being renowned locally for the great relationships Sian and Neil form with the people they work with. This includes the regular staff, some of whom are sixth form students who come to gain work experience while studying, but often return in their holidays having enjoyed the job so much! The atmosphere at Foxy's welcomes everyone with open arms and makes the café an ideal venue for a natter, a Welsh lesson or a club meeting over a delicious lunch, breakfast or coffee and cake, freshly made by Mr Foxy himself.

Foxy's Deli and Café stands out to everyone who drops by for its quirkiness and strong commitment to buying and shopping local. Sian and Neil have worked hard to achieve the vision they started out with, moving with the times but keeping it homemade, tasty and Welsh through and through.

chocolate
brownie
cheesecake
£3.00

FOXY'S

Foxy's Deli and Café
WELSH RAREBIT BURGER

We wanted to create a Welsh dish with a twist, so this burger was developed to combine two really classic comfort foods into one delicious surprise!

Preparation time: 20 minutes | Cooking time: approx. 1 hour 30 minutes | Serves: 4

Ingredients

For the rarebit burgers:

700g mature cheddar, grated

150ml milk

25g plain flour

50g breadcrumbs

1 tbsp English mustard powder

Good dash of Worcestershire sauce

A few drops of Tabasco sauce (optional)

2 eggs

2 egg yolks

1 large white onion

700g lean minced beef (5-10% fat)

For the onion marmalade:

2kg red onions

4 cloves of garlic

140g butter

4 tbsp olive oil

140g golden caster sugar

1 tbsp fresh thyme leaves, finely chopped

Pinch of chilli flakes (optional)

1 bottle of red wine

350ml sherry vinegar or red wine vinegar

200ml Port

For the baked potato wedges:

4 baking potatoes

Oil

Salt and pepper

Method

For the rarebit burger

Put the cheese in a pan with the milk. Slowly melt the cheese, but do not allow the milk to boil or the cheese will separate. When the mixture is smooth, add the flour, breadcrumbs and mustard. Cook over a low heat, stirring continuously, until the mixture forms a ball which comes off the sides of the pan. Add the Worcestershire sauce and the Tabasco sauce if using, season with salt and pepper and then leave the mixture to cool.

When cool, put the mixture in a food processor and beat it, slowly adding the eggs and yolks. If you don't have a food processor you can do this by hand with a wooden spoon. Finely dice the onion, add it to the minced beef in a separate bowl and season well. Using a food processor or your hands, combine the beef mixture with 200g of the rarebit mixture. Form the burger mix into four patties. The remaining rarebit mixture can be frozen for later use if you're only making four burgers. Pan fry or oven bake the patties until cooked through when all the other elements are ready.

For the onion marmalade

Halve and thinly slice the onions and garlic. Melt the butter with the oil in a large, heavy-based saucepan over a high heat. Tip in the onions and garlic and give them a good stir in the butter so they are glossy. Sprinkle over the sugar, thyme leaves, chilli flakes if using and some salt and pepper. Give everything another really good stir and reduce the heat slightly. Cook uncovered for 40-50 minutes, stirring occasionally. Slow cooking is the secret of really soft and sticky onions, so don't rush this part. The onions are ready when all their juices have evaporated; they're really soft and sticky and smell of caramelised sugar. They should be so soft that they break when pressed against the side of the pan with a wooden spoon. At this stage, pour in the wine, vinegar and Port. Simmer over a high heat for 25-30 minutes without covering, stirring every so often until the onions are a deep mahogany colour and the liquid has reduced by about two-thirds. The marmalade is done when drawing a spoon across the bottom of the pan clears a path that fills rapidly with syrupy juice. Leave the marmalade to cool in the pan, then scoop into sterilised jars and seal. Can be eaten straight away, but keeps in the fridge for up to 3 months.

For the baked potato wedges

Place the four baking potatoes in the oven for 1½ to 2 hours, depending on their size. When cooked, cool the potatoes until they can be sliced into wedge shapes. Heat some oil with a pinch of salt and pepper in a pan in the oven until sizzling hot. Place the wedges in the pan and roast until crispy.

To serve

Use buns or rolls of your choice to build the burger. Slice the bread in half and toast both sides. Spread some onion marmalade on the bottom half, add the burger and sandwich with the top half. Serve with the baked potato wedges and a dressed side salad.

Where to BE-GIN

The welcoming atmosphere and irresistible produce at Ginhaus Deli is testament to the love affair with food and gin that started and continued within its walls.

Kate and Mike were already looking for a change of direction when opportunity knocked in the shape of a former deli that was closing its doors in Llandeilo. With Mike's brother as the owner of the building and Mike's own background as a builder, it wasn't long (four weeks, to be exact) before a transformation of the whole ground floor was complete. The couple managed to get everything ready in time for the opening of Ginhaus Deli to coincide with their 10 year anniversary, a nod to their new beginning as well as the past, since their premises were once the Three Tuns, a much loved and frequented village pub where Mike and Kate first met.

To one side of the inviting space is a deli section stocked with Welsh produce and fresh food to take away. Cheeses, cooked meats, homemade quiches, Scotch eggs and other savoury bites complement a range of homemade cakes and, of course, gins. If the 'gin wall' displaying over three hundred bottles of gin varieties doesn't tempt customers over into the bar and seating area, nothing will! The incredible range is topped up by the hundred or so on pour behind the bar for an afternoon G&T or an evening cocktail and the 'tasting boards' that hold a monthly rotation of three gins to try. Ginhaus opens late on Fridays and Saturdays, extending its super relaxed atmosphere into the evenings with pizza made in-house and topped with goodies from around the deli.

The name and main theme of Mike and Kate's deli emerged from research into the area, when they discovered that there had been a distillery on their street. "Some people come in every day, including a dog that loves our croissants!" says Kate, and it's that element of putting a smile on everyone's face that makes it such a lovely place to work and come back to, as many of the university students do over summer. They even work with one of Mike's former colleagues, who swapped the building site for the on-site kitchen! Drawing on their own experiences and the strength of Llandeilo's community has been part of the Ginhaus team's aim, bringing people together over lovely Coaltown coffee, local produce like charcuterie from The Baker's Pig, and of course plenty of gin!

Ginhaus
ABER FALLS ORANGE MARMALADE GIN & POPPY SEED CAKE

Combining our two passions – gin and cake – this marmalade gin and poppy seed cake is never on the bar for long! Aber Falls distillery, located in Abergwyngregyn in North Wales, produces whiskey as well as a premium range of small batch, hand-crafted gins and liqueurs. Their Orange Marmalade Gin has a refined balance of sweet and bitter orange flavours.

Preparation time: 30 minutes | Cooking time: 1 hour | Serves: 10

Ingredients

For the cake:

4 tbsp thick-cut marmalade

215g softened butter

215g caster sugar

280g self-raising flour

1 tsp baking powder

4 large eggs

1 large orange, zested

2 tbsp poppy seeds

125ml full-fat milk

50ml lemon juice

For the sugar syrup:

25ml Aber Falls Orange Marmalade Gin (this is the gin that we use and recommend, but of course you can substitute with a gin of your choice, or omit if preferred)

1 orange, juiced

55g caster sugar

For the topping:

2 tbsp thick-cut marmalade

25ml Aber Falls Orange Marmalade Gin

5 blood orange crisps (or 1 fresh blood (or regular) orange, thinly sliced)

1 tsp poppy seeds

Method

For the cake

Preheat the oven to 160°c. Grease and line a 900g (2lb) loaf tin. Put the marmalade into a small pan and heat gently until melted. Set aside to cool. Cream the butter and sugar together until light and fluffy. Sieve the flour and baking powder together. Beat in the eggs one at a time, adding a spoonful of the flour mixture with each egg. Add the remaining ingredients and stir until well combined. Pour into the prepared tin and bake for 1 hour, covering with parchment after 45 minutes. When done, leave the cake in the tin and prick the top all over with a skewer or cocktail stick.

For the sugar syrup

Place the sugar syrup ingredients in a small pan and gently warm until the sugar is dissolved. Slowly pour over the cake while hot, and then leave the cake to cool completely. When the cake has cooled, remove from the tin.

For the topping

Place the marmalade and gin in a small pan and gently warm until melted and combined. Spoon the topping over the cake. Sprinkle with poppy seeds and decorate with blood orange crisps.

Littoral LUXURY

Holm House Hotel and Spa embodies the tranquillity of a coastal retreat, complete with warm attentive service and of course, fantastic food and drink.

From the dining, to the twelve boutique rooms, to the fully appointed spa, the ultimate aim of the committed team at Holm House Hotel and Spa is to provide guests – whether they stay for a week or visit for an afternoon – with a warm, friendly, welcoming experience filled with relaxation and great taste in every sense of the word! Dan Jones is the general manager and emphasises the importance of guests "feeling totally comfortable and being able to treat yourself" on any occasion.

With its sea views and proximity to the centre of Cardiff, the Penarth location lends itself to utilising the best of land and sea. This is reflected inside the spa, hotel and restaurant today but also harks back to the building's history as a private residence, built in the 1920s by a successful industrialist who was the son of a fishing magnate. Nine of the twelve rooms look out over the Bristol Channel and include subtle touches in the décor that nod to the coastline and the period alongside contemporary flair. When it comes to wining and dining, or setting you up for a day of indulgence, Holm House isn't short of stylish spaces to suit all its visitors. There's a lounge, snug, a cocktail bar with expert mixologists on hand, and a private dining room as well as the large, light-filled restaurant which

extends into a beautiful terrace in the cliff top garden.

The kitchen's repertoire covers flavoursome breakfasts, lunches, afternoon teas, à la carte dinners and even weekend barbecues. Matt Owen, the head chef at Holm House, uses a variety of locally sourced produce and top quality ingredients at their seasonal best from around the UK, from Welsh dry-aged beef to Cornish turbot, and morel, girolle and Chanterelle mushrooms to the freshest black truffle from Italy and France. He carefully develops the restaurant menu around the produce on offer to extract vibrant flavours and textures and deliver a range of inspired dishes.

Dan describes Holm House as having "a lot of local support" which, as keen advocates for the south west region of Wales and their own beautiful spot on its coastline, he and his staff are really proud of. They have even linked up with local artists, whose works adorn the hotel walls and are also available for visitors to purchase. He, Matt and spa manager Abigail Beynon are always striving for improvement, ensuring that Holm House continues to offer an experience of the Welsh coast you'll want to repeat again and again!

Holm House Hotel and Spa

Holm House Hotel and Spa

LEMON, HERB AND PINE NUT CRUSTED FILLET OF TURBOT

For this dish we use fresh wild Scottish or Irish Sea cod if it's going on the lunch menu. For dinner, only the finest wild Cornish or Scottish Turbot will do! You can choose any good quality white fish to use at home though; we'd recommend asking your fishmonger what's best on the day.

Preparation time: 15 minutes | Cooking time: approx. 35 minutes | Serves: 2

Ingredients

2x 230g fillets of turbot (or white fish of your choice)

Drizzle of pomace oil

For the crust:

A handful of parsley

A handful of tarragon

A handful of chervil

1 tsp garlic purée

100ml olive oil

100g unsalted butter

300g breadcrumbs

1-2 lemons, zested and juiced

50g pine nuts, roughly chopped

For the parsley sauce:

1 bunch of curly leaf parsley

1 banana shallot, finely diced

1 tbsp garlic purée

200ml white wine

300ml double cream

For the accompaniments:

1 head of fennel

Drizzle of extra-virgin olive oil

Knob of butter

Salt and pepper

1 sprig of thyme

1 clove of garlic, crushed

1 lemon, sliced

3-4 leaves of Swiss chard

Pinch of freshly grated nutmeg

Small handful of red-veined sorrel leaves

Method

Preheat the oven to 180°c

Portion the fillets into two or three pieces each. Place the fish on a tray and drizzle with pomace oil. Season with salt and pepper and then set aside while you make the crust. Place everything except the pine nuts in a blender and blend until fine. Add the chopped pine nuts and mix well. Cook the fish in the oven for 3 minutes and then take it out and remove the skin. Cover the fish with the crust and cook in the oven for a further 3-4 minutes.

For the parsley sauce

First bring a pan of water to the boil. Drop in the parsley to cook for 20 seconds and then transfer it straight into a bowl of iced water. Leave to cool completely. Sauté the shallot and garlic in olive oil and a small knob of butter for 3-5 minutes. Deglaze the pan with white wine and reduce by half. Add the double cream and cook out until the mixture has thickened; another 3-5 minutes. Squeeze all the water out of the parsley and add it to the pan. Immediately transfer the sauce to a blender and blitz until smooth; add more cream if needed to get a good pouring consistency. You should end up with a beautifully bright green parsley sauce.

For the accompaniments

Cut the fennel bulb into quarters, leaving the stem on. Drizzle with extra-virgin olive oil and add a knob of butter, a pinch of salt and pepper, the thyme and garlic. Cover the fennel with lemon slices and then roast at about 160°c until softened and golden brown. This will take around 35 minutes, depending on the size of the fennel.

Slice the Swiss chard leaves lengthways and sauté in a pan with a small knob of butter. Season with salt, pepper and a little freshly grated nutmeg.

To serve

Finely slice some of the sorrel and scatter over the chard. Plate the fish, fennel, chard and parsley sauce and garnish with a few whole leaves of sorrel.

PERL LAS CHEESE BONBONS WITH HONEYCOMB, PEAR AND PORT LEMONADE

This dish is a play on a cheeseboard, with the big bold flavour of Welsh Perl Las blue cheese, beautiful sweet pure honeycomb, crisp fresh pear and smooth pear purée. All this is washed down with a sweet and refreshing homemade Port lemonade. A fantastic start or end to any meal!

Preparation time: 30 minutes, plus chilling time | Cooking time: approx. 30 minutes | Serves: 6-8

Ingredients

1 pure bee honeycomb

For the bonbons:

250g Perl Las blue cheese, crumbled

150g potato, boiled and mashed

100g walnuts, roughly chopped

200g plain flour, seasoned with salt

5 eggs, beaten

400g panko breadcrumbs

1 tbsp black onion seeds

For the pear purée:

1kg pears

100g caster sugar

100ml water

For the Port lemonade:

200ml lemon juice

200ml mineral water or if preferred sparkling water

200g caster sugar

Splash of Port, to taste

Method

To make the bonbons, combine the blue cheese, potato and walnuts thoroughly and shape into 20g balls. You should have about 25 of these (enough for a party!). Leave in the fridge to firm up. Once set, pane the bonbons by rolling each ball in seasoned flour, then dipping into the beaten egg – making sure it's completely covered – and then rolling in breadcrumbs mixed with the black onion seeds.

For the pear purée

First peel, deseed and roughly chop all the pears. Place all the ingredients into a pan and cover. Bring to the boil, and then remove the lid once boiling and cook out until the pears are soft. When the fruit has all broken down and starts to look like apple sauce, it's ready to blitz. Use a stick blender or blender to purée and then pass the mixture through a sieve to get a silky smooth texture.

For the Port lemonade

Combine the lemon juice with the water and add sugar to taste, depending on how tart you'd like the drink to be. Stir well and then mix in the Port, again to taste. Chill in the fridge until everything else is ready.

To serve

Brush a swirl of pear purée onto the plate just off centre. Add three dots of purée to the plate for the bonbons to sit on. Crumble over a few small pieces of honeycomb. Deep fry the bonbons in small batches until golden brown. Remove from the fryer and drain on kitchen paper before serving. Add some slices of fresh pear to garnish and serve with a shot glass of the Port lemonade on the side.

In it
TOGETHER

With a passion for food, James Sommerin combines his family heritage with Michelin-starred fine dining on the seafront in Penarth.

A proud a family-orientated restaurant, Restaurant James Sommerin was set up in 2014 by James, who had always dreamt of owning his own establishment. Having worked in restaurants since the age of 12, his love of cooking was inspired by his late grandmother and many Saturdays spent cooking with her. After moving to Scotland when he was 16 to work in a hotel, he fell in love with Louise, now his wife, who works front of house in the restaurant with him. To James' immense pleasure, his eldest daughter has followed in his footsteps. Georgia has been working closely with him in the kitchen since the age of 13 and was recently promoted to senior chef de partie.

With such a devoted team behind him, James can safely say that all the food is "cooked with love". The restaurant runs both an à la carte and a tasting menu, which can be either six or nine course. The different courses in the tasting menu can vary widely, as James uses only the best ingredients they have in on the day. 95% of the ingredients sourced by the restaurant are local, coming from suppliers based in South Wales. The menu changes seasonally, but the firm favourite that took James to the Great British Menu final, his famous liquid pea ravioli, stays on all year round.

In addition to the main dining area, the restaurant offers a chef's table where you can eat in the heart of the kitchen and watch your 14-course meal being cooked right in front of you. James aspires to create a welcoming and unpretentious atmosphere, and the soul of his kitchen is the purpose-built stove; he designed the restaurant from scratch around this centrepiece after falling for the seafront location. The dining area was built to be light and airy with a relaxed vibe, with windows looking out over the estuary. From the very beginning of their creation, James and his family have worked by his ethos "you're only as good as the service you're in". Looking towards the future, he and his family team strive to make every day better than the last, creating a real impact on the world of food with true flavour and genuine passion.

JAMES SOMMERIN

Restaurant James Sommerin

WELSH LAMB WITH BROAD BEANS, TURNIP AND CUMIN

It was a no-brainer putting this dish on the menu. As a Welsh restaurant, having Welsh lamb on the menu is a must. Lamb is my favourite meat and I also love to cook with it. Treat it with the respect it deserves; make sure it's cooked slowly to ensure the meat is tender and falls apart.

Preparation time: 1 hour | Cooking time: 12 hours | Serves: 4

Ingredients

For the turnip purée:

1kg turnips, peeled

500ml milk

100ml cream and 100g butter

For the broad beans:

20g butter

1 tsp chopped thyme

1 clove of garlic, chopped

120g fresh broad beans, outer skins removed

For the cumin sauce:

100g lamb fat

200g lamb trimmings

1 onion, sliced

1 tsp cumin seeds

1 stick of celery, sliced

1 tsp smoked paprika

2 sprigs of tarragon

200ml Madeira

1 litre lamb stock

½ litre chicken stock

For the lamb:

4 50g lamb breasts

20g rendered lamb fat

1 sprig of rosemary

To assemble:

400g lamb loin

20g lamb fat

Turnip

Nasturtium leaves

Method

For the turnip purée

Thinly slice the turnips and place in a pan. Add the milk, cream and butter, then bring to the boil and cook until soft. Strain, reserving the cooking liquid, and blend in a Thermomix with the temperature setting at 90°c. Add the cooking liquid back in until the purée is the required texture. Cook for longer in the Thermomix to get a smoother consistency.

For the broad beans

Emulsify the butter with 10ml of water. Add the thyme and garlic, then warm the broad beans through at the last minute.

For the cumin sauce

In a pan, heat the lamb fat and add the trimmings, onion and cumin. Cook for 2 minutes until there is good colouration. Add the celery, paprika and tarragon, then deglaze with Madeira. Reduce the liquid by three-quarters. Add the stocks and reduce to the required consistency, then pass through a fine sieve.

For the lamb

Place the lamb breasts in a vacuum pack bag with the lamb fat and a sprig of rosemary. Cook at 80°c for 12 hours on a steam setting. Remove once cooked and then press under a weight. Allow to cool.

To assemble

Pan fry the loin of lamb in 20g of lamb fat. Add the breasts and caramelise evenly. Place the turnip purée on a plate and build the meat and broad beans on top. Thinly slice some raw turnip and season with salt and a little olive oil. Place the turnip slices on top and finish with nasturtium leaves and cumin sauce.

Fusion FREEDOM

Inspired by his father, Indian-born chef Stephen Gomes prides himself on creating innovative and authentic Indian food with a Welsh twist at his multi award-winning restaurant.

With three generations of chefs in his family, Stephen had all the talent and inspiration to take the culinary world on. When he finished his training in Mumbai, he travelled all over the world – including Dubai, the Middle East, Europe, South Africa and America – soaking up the cuisine and culture before finally settling in Wales in 2004. Since doing so, he has won many awards for his food, including an AA rosette for his restaurant Moksh.

Moksh's name comes from the Sanskrit word for freedom or liberation and the restaurant showcases Stephen's individual and inventive style; a mixture of authentic Indian cuisine and modern gastrophysics. Drawing inspiration from his travels, the menu combines an eclectic mix of modern flair and authentic ingredients, with that all-important Welsh twist in evidence too. The chefs make the most of the fresh produce on their doorstep, from dairy and vegetables to the favoured Welsh lamb that takes a starring role in many of their dishes. The menu is vibrant, with traditional dishes, some British favourites and Moksh's speciality curries, all presented in modern and colourful ways.

With the combination of fine dining and a relaxed atmosphere, Moksh is a favourite in Cardiff. For Stephen it's not just about the food; Moksh offers a full dining experience. From the eye-catching presentation to the quirky and catchy names of the dishes – Mystical Garden being just one example; a dessert mingling carefully balanced spice with delicately sweet meringue and mousse – the restaurant creates an atmosphere for people who not only enjoy great food, but enjoy the whole process of going out to a restaurant and being wowed by the show. The food is all the entertainment you'll need.

Moksh was born from a genuine love of food and a passion for sharing flavour with others. As a chef, Stephen thrives on creating new and exciting dishes, infusing his restaurant with that positivity. The restaurant's success shows that customers are intrigued by his contemporary take on authenticity. Moksh will be moving to a new venue in the near future just across the road, offering more space to expand and develop the already popular ideas that spring from Stephen's fun and inventive take on the food he loves.

Moksh
LAMB RAILWAY CURRY

This is one of Stephen's favourite recipes and was a popular dish in the time of his great grandfather, who was head chef at the Eastern Shipping Company in the days of the Raj; the railway curry was considered aristocratic and served on the Indian railways.

Preparation time: 5 minutes | Cook time: 25 minutes | Serves: 4

Ingredients

125ml oil

2 cinnamon sticks

1 whole nutmeg

4 green cardamom pods

2½ tsp ginger and garlic paste

900g lamb, cut into boneless cubes

Salt, to taste

400g onion, finely chopped

1 tsp red chilli powder

¾ tsp garam masala

1½ tsp coriander powder

1 tsp turmeric powder

225g tomato purée

50g yoghurt

940ml water

2 tsp fresh coriander, chopped

1 tsp roasted cumin

Method

Begin by heating the oil in a large pan, and then add the cinnamon, nutmeg, and cardamom and sauté until they crackle. Add the ginger and garlic paste and fry for a further 5 minutes. Next, add the lamb cubes and chopped onions. Cook on a medium heat until any moisture dries out and then add salt, the chilli powder, garam masala, coriander, and turmeric. Stir in the tomato purée and the yoghurt and cook for 2 minutes, then add the water. Rogan oil should appear during this stage; this occurs when the onion and spices are fried in oil, and takes approximately 2 minutes after the yoghurt has been added. Reduce the heat and cook until the lamb pieces are tender and the curry thickens, and then remove it from the heat.

To serve

Transfer the curry to a serving dish and garnish with the fresh coriander and roasted cumin seeds. This dish is traditionally served hot with bread or dinner rolls.

Down on THE FARM

The Moody Sow is the latest addition to the long-established Cefn Mably Farm Park, where top-quality butchery, freshly baked deli goods and the very best of Welsh and British farm produce always draw a hungry crowd!

A farm shop stocked full of delicious Welsh and British pork, beef, lamb, chicken and much more seemed like a natural progression for the family-run Cefn Mably Farm Park. The expansion began in 2013 and involved almost two years of building work which everyone pitched in to complete, to get the shop open for its first weekend. The success of that first venture has since grown steadily, with awards won for the burgers, sausages, Scotch eggs and lots of the butchery, awarded by the Q Guild, Great Taste and other nationally recognised bodies.

The Moody Sow follows in the footsteps of the current generation's great-great-great grandfather and his brother, who were a farmer and butcher team in the early 1900s with shops in the Cardiff and Rumney markets. Today it is overseen by Anthony Tilbury, whose mother-in-law set up the park over twenty years ago and after whom he tells us the farm shop is categorically not named… The team comprises Anthony and his wife Tina, his brother-in-law Rhys Edwards and Rhys' wife Alyona. Head butcher Chris Regan and his apprentice Ethan Ford are now in charge of the meat counter, while Adrian Vlad and Alex Rees cook all the fresh deli counter products on site and recently Jack Ford has also brought a wealth of knowledge to the team.

You'll only find Welsh and British meat at the butchery counter, all of which comes to the farm shop still attached to its animal! When they're not sourcing from neighbouring farms (the closest is barely a mile down the road) The Moody Sow team use small independent specialist outsourcers who visit the farms, meet the farmers and choose the products themselves. They age the meat on the bone themselves, as well as curing their own bacon and creating a range of award-winning burgers and sausages, and the deli counter has a range of pies, pasties, sausage rolls, Scotch eggs and other foods ready to take away.

In addition to the counters, customers can stock up on fresh and frozen fruit and vegetables, dairy, locally made preserves, regional beers and freshly baked bread – and all this after enjoying a spot of lunch in the café or on the south-facing terrace – which pretty much makes the Moody Sow a paradise for anyone who loves good homemade food! The returning customers say it all, thanks to the emphasis on quality that Anthony is so committed to, and sticking with the best produce around means everyone's happy whether they get to sell or buy it.

Moody Sow Farm Shop
EUGENE'S MEATBALLS

These meatballs are one of my favourite recipes and the sauce is simply delicious. This is a great alternative to spaghetti Bolognese and a hearty family meal, especially served with homemade garlic bread and pasta cooked al dente. You'll be going back for seconds!

Preparation time: 45 minutes | Cooking time: approx. 1 hour | Serves: 12

Ingredients

For the meatballs:

500g minced pork

500g minced beef

2 fresh free-range eggs

100g Parmesan, grated

80g breadcrumbs

6-8 cloves of garlic, minced

2 tsp dried oregano

2 tsp dried marjoram

2 tsp dried basil

1 tsp salt

Freshly ground black pepper, to taste

For the tomato sauce:

2 large onions

6-8 cloves of garlic

1 tsp oregano

1 tsp marjoram

Knob of butter

Glug of olive oil

1.38kg passata (2 large bottles)

Pinch of sugar

1 tsp salt

1 tsp ground black pepper

200ml full-fat milk

Method

For the meatballs

Place all the ingredients for the meatballs in a bowl and mix well. We usually grind the herbs into a powder before adding them, but you don't have to do this and can also adjust the amount and type of herbs used. Form the mixture into balls about the size of a squash ball. The amounts given should make roughly 100 meatballs.

For the sauce

First blend the onion, garlic and herbs to a pulp in a food processor. Heat the butter and oil in a pan, add the blitzed sauce base and cook very slowly with a lid on until soft. Keep checking it though as it sweats to make sure it doesn't catch and burn. When done, add half of the passata (one bottle) and if you want to make a lot of sauce add the rest. Half fill one of the passata bottles with hot water, swill it around to incorporate all the remaining tomato goodness, and add this to pan with the pinch of sugar, salt and pepper. Cook the sauce out for about 10-15 minutes. Then add the milk and gently drop the meatballs in. Do not stir until the meatballs have browned a bit, as they will fall apart if you push them around too soon. Cook for another 20 minutes or so, check the flavour and add more seasoning if needed. The sauce shouldn't be too runny so keep the pan on the heat until it has thickened up and the meatballs are cooked through.

To serve

Sit back and enjoy. Boom.

Moody Sow Farm Shop
SCOTCH EGG

When we initially decided to make the Scotch eggs for the shop, we were going to use a standard breadcrumb for the coating. However, on the day we had some day-old bread left over and used that instead, which created a coarse breadcrumb and has actually given our eggs a very unique look and taste!

Preparation time: 10 minutes | Cooking time: 20 minutes | Serves: 1 (the recipe can easily be multiplied)

Ingredients

1 medium free-range egg

150g sausage meat from your choice of Moody Sow sausages

15g flavouring, e.g. black pudding (optional)

1 small free-range egg, beaten

Fresh breadcrumbs (use coarse crumbs for a crispier coating)

Method

Firstly, boil the medium-sized egg for 8 minutes. Take 150g of sausage meat and combine it with any other ingredients you'd like to flavour the Scotch egg with, such as black pudding, sweet chilli sauce, diced apple or finely chopped fresh herbs. We use 10% of the amount of sausage meat for flavourings, so for this recipe you would need 15g of your chosen addition. Wrap the boiled egg in the flavoured sausage meat and mould with your hands to make it roughly spherical. Dip the Scotch egg in beaten egg and then roll gently in breadcrumbs.

To cook, preheat a deep fat fryer to 170°c. Lower the Scotch egg into the hot oil and cook for 10 minutes until the coating is nice and crispy. Leave it to drain on kitchen paper for a few minutes.

To serve

Serve the Scotch eggs while still slightly warm, and be prepared to be praised for your culinary masterpiece.

Bread of HEAVEN

One Mile Bakery is a revolutionary way of getting the freshest bread, along with homemade soups and preserves, from the kitchen it's made in to the people of Cardiff.

Nick Macleod wanted to find a way to combine his passion for baking with a livelihood to follow his career as a professional rugby player. An opportunity arose to take over the reins of the flagship One Mile Bakery, so he moved back home from Manchester and began making and delivering his own bread, soups and preserves. He has successfully run the micro bakery since 2016, delivering to his local customers in Rhiwbina and teaching over 300 people how to make beautiful, homemade bread.

"I've absolutely loved bread since I was little," says Nick, who was influenced by his food-loving family, especially his grandmother's baking, from a young age. The breads Nick delivers to the doors of his customers are classic or sourdough loaves, depending on the chosen subscription, paired with a soup and preserve if they like. His own classes are a regular feature of the weekly calendar, and are invariably fully booked due to their popularity and enthusiastic reviews! All taught by Nick, the workshops cover a variety of bread-making, from sourdough to croissants, and focaccia to festive bakes. Nick enjoys foraging for the diverse ingredients used in his creations – such as wild garlic from nearby woodland – and is even lucky enough to have a keen fruit and veg grower for a neighbour!

Seasonality and sustainability, two important words when it comes to One Mile Bakery's ethos, go hand in hand for Nick. His packaging is all recyclable and his method of transport is his bike, which combined with the subscription method means there's a no-waste approach that works on the homely scale One Mile Bakery is sticking to. "There has been a real renaissance in people wanting good-quality bread," says Nick. He is only too happy to oblige, producing tasty and interesting food and passing on the skills to make it, in a down-to-earth manner that's all about celebrating lovely local food.

One Mile Bakery
WILD GARLIC FOCACCIA

This is a brilliant and delicious way to showcase the versatility of wild garlic. We are very lucky to have the woods of North Cardiff carpeted in wild garlic throughout the spring. The scent will instantly give it away, so it's a great one to start with for the foraging novice.

Preparation time: approx. 2 hours | Cooking time: approx. 20 minutes | Serves: 8

Ingredients

For the wild garlic oil:

50g wild garlic leaves

100ml olive oil

For the focaccia:

500g strong white bread flour

10g salt

10g fresh yeast / 7g instant / 5g fast dried yeast

375g warm water

40g olive oil

Method

For the wild garlic oil

Thoroughly wash the leaves and pat them dry. Roughly chop and mix with the olive oil. Blend using a hand blender or a food processor until you have a bright green oil. Pour into a sterilised jar.

For the focaccia

Weigh the flour, salt and yeast into a large mixing bowl, being careful to keep the salt and yeast on separate sides of the bowl. Make a well in the middle of the flour and add the water and oil. Mix all the ingredients together in the bowl until all the dry flour has been incorporated into the mix, and then knead on a clean work surface for 10 minutes. (Don't be tempted to flour the work surface for the kneading stage; persevere with the slack dough…you will get better bread for it!) Place back into a lightly oiled bowl, then cover with oiled cling film and leave to rise until doubled in size. Preheat the oven to 220°c.

Tip the dough out into a lightly oiled, deep sided baking tray and then using your fingertips gently stretch to the size of your baking tray, working the dough out like a pizza base until it's about 1cm thick. Then pour on 3-4 tablespoons of the wild garlic oil, smoothing it over the surface, and press light dimples into the dough. Cover and leave for another 60 minutes or until roughly doubled in size. When proved, bake the focaccia in the preheated oven for 18-22 minutes. Remove the focaccia from the baking tray, checking the bottom sounds hollow when tapped. If not, place back into the oven, out of the tin, for a further 5 minutes and check again. Place on a wire rack to cool and brush liberally with more wild garlic oil while still warm, then tuck in!

A shining EXAMPLE

One of Cardiff's newest restaurants, Seren Diemwnt, aims to combine fine food with affordability and establish itself as part of the community in Llandaff.

The owner, founder and head chef of one of Cardiff's newest independent restaurants, Gethin Rees, has taken the next big step in a career driven by a long-standing passion for cooking to open Seren Diemwnt. Meaning diamond star, the dining destination places emphasis on simply serving great food for everyone to enjoy; inclusivity and accessibility are important to Gethin and his small team. They are all committed to providing each guest with the best experience possible, and this family feel – where the seven members of staff all have input – along with support from his partner and family has helped Gethin to create a welcoming yet sophisticated restaurant for the Llandaff community and beyond as its reputation grows.

The ambitious chef is Cardiff born and bred, so taking the leap of faith to start his own business in his home city made the achievement even more special. His aim was always to open his own venue by the age of 32; Gethin's 32nd birthday in March 2018 came five months after Seren Diemwnt served its first customers, so it's safe to say he can tick that off the bucket list! He has enjoyed having the freedom to develop his own recipes, tweaking the ideas that might come from dining out elsewhere or inspiration from the seasonal produce around him to get the balance just right.

The menu is an à la carte offering heading towards the fine dining end of the spectrum, but for Gethin that level of quality shouldn't mean the food becomes vastly expensive and therefore exclusive. He also ensures that there are plenty of vegetarian options and around 80% of the menu is gluten-free. His aim is to make Seren Diemwnt a great place to eat out for everyone, not just on the rare occasion it's affordable but for any celebration or evening out. A lot of work went into making the interior contemporary and stylish during renovations of the venue, which now features soft lighting and candles on the tables to create a really special atmosphere.

Gethin's vision for the future focuses on first establishing Seren Diemwnt as a part of the Llandaff high street community, which will stem from the friendly welcome his team always offer customers – recognised when they return and made to feel really at home when they visit for the first time – and the care the restaurant puts into each aspect of its unique dining experience.

Seren Diemwnt
HERB AND GARLIC ROAST POLENTA WITH BEETROOT CRISPS AND FONDANT POTATO

This dish is something I love due to the contrast of colours and the simplistic nature of it once everything is made in advance. The dish came to me from a few other dishes I have created and also trying to cater for more vegans and gluten-free individuals as it's an area many restaurants overlook.

Preparation time: approx. 30 minutes | Cooking time: approx. 45 minutes | Serves: 4-5

Ingredients

For the polenta:

1 banana shallot, finely diced

2 cloves of garlic, finely diced

4 sprigs of thyme, leaves picked and diced

Dash of olive oil

750ml vegetable stock or water

50ml white wine

200g polenta powder

Salt and pepper

For the fondant potato:

2 Maris Piper potatoes

2 sprigs of rosemary, leaves picked and diced

3 cloves of garlic, diced

200g butter

For the beetroot crisps:

3 red beetroot, cooked

2 cloves of garlic, finely diced

2 sprigs of thyme

For the baby gem dressing:

1 baby gem lettuce

200g spinach

25ml olive oil

To plate:

100g shiitake mushrooms, washed

Knob of butter

1 clove of garlic, minced

A handful of fresh spinach, washed

Method

For the polenta

Slightly fry the shallot, garlic and thyme in a dash of olive oil then add the stock or water and the white wine to the pan. Add the polenta, season, and cook out on a medium heat for 5 and a half minutes, stirring continually to stop the mix sticking. The polenta should be quite like dough. Let it cool slightly and then transfer onto a baking mat or tray covered with greaseproof paper. Using a ring cutter, portion out four or five rounds of the polenta. Place the cut out polenta into the oven (on the mat or tray) and cook at 170°c for around 10-14 minutes until slightly crispy.

For the fondant potato

Peel the potatoes and then using an apple corer, press through each potato to get potato cylinders (around 4 from each potato). Level off the ends of each cylinder for neat presentation. Lightly fry the potatoes in a non-stick pan and cook until lightly coloured, then sprinkle with salt and pepper, rosemary and garlic. Add the butter to the pan, cover with foil then cook in the oven at 180°c for around 10-12 minutes.

For the beetroot crisps

Thinly slice the beetroot and sprinkle with garlic, thyme and seasoning. Drizzle a little olive oil over the slices and lay them on a tray covered with greaseproof paper or a baking mat. Cook in the oven at 145°c for 18-25 minutes until slightly crispy, and then take out and leave to finish drying.

For the baby gem dressing

Drop the baby gem and spinach into a pan of boiling water and then take out after 45 seconds. Cool down and then dry off the leaves. Blend them with the olive oil and season to taste.

To plate

Warm the polenta cakes and potato fondants through in the oven with a small amount of butter. Pan fry the mushrooms with more butter and the minced garlic. Add the spinach and season. Place a polenta cake in the middle of each plate, spoon the mushroom and spinach mix over the top, add the potato fondants and beetroot crisps, and finally drizzle the dressing over everything.

Little saucepans,
BIG DREAMS

Head chef Andrew Sheridan's enthusiasm for using the best of Welsh produce to create dishes everyone will love infuses Sosban with a unique sense of fun and personal connection to food in south west Wales.

In the summer of 2017, Andrew Sheridan and his close-knit team of chefs came to Llanelli with big ambitions and piles of enthusiasm. They were up for a challenge, turning the existing restaurant into a culinary experience by throwing out the stuffy formalities of fine dining and simply serving food that was delicious, recognisable and accessible to absolutely everyone.

Sosban emphasises the personal connection we all have with certain dishes – for Andrew that's childhood memories of fish and chips, for his sous chef Jake it's fresh mackerel barbecued on the coals down at the beach – and recreates those familiar flavours with technical skill and modern creativity. Sam, Ryan, Joe and Dan complete the kitchen team, who all work together on developing the restaurant menus based on the very best produce they can get, all sourced within 50 miles. Using seasonal vegetables is crucial to updating the dishes according to the time of year, building flavour and texture around a top-quality core ingredient. Visiting farms, foraging, mushroom picking and discussing dry aging times with the butcher are all part of the day-to-day involvement Andrew

and his chefs have in choosing and preparing the ingredients they work with.

Making sure this translates to the person eating the food at the table is really important to Andrew, so at Sosban it's the chefs rather than waiters who bring the dishes out. The passion and intimate knowledge they each have for everything on the 7 or 9 course tasting menu, à la carte menu and the Kid's Board – featuring the best burger and triple-cooked chips most children will have ever eaten – means that explaining dishes and educating guests comes easily. The experience is designed to ensure that no one feels out of place or afraid of trying something new, which is complemented beautifully by the relaxed elegance of the exposed brick-and-beam interior.

Andrew has his sights on a Michelin star in the near future. Sosban is thoroughly embracing the challenge of creating a unique legacy in south west Wales as well as gaining a reputation for innovation across the country. "This is all about the food we love cooking," says Andrew, "and if we can make the little things amazing, think what we can do with the bigger things!"

Sosban

Sosban

APPLE RICE PUDDING, HAY ICE CREAM AND CARAMELISED MILK SKIN

This recipe's incredible heritage stretches back almost 80 years. It came down to Andrew from his great-grandmother, who worked in a hospital during World War Two and made the first version of this apple rice pudding with fruit from the farm she lived on, to bring in for her patients.

Preparation time: 45 minutes | Cook time: 1 hour 50 minutes | Serves: 4

Ingredients

For the rice pudding:

60g pudding rice

425ml milk

140ml double cream

30g sugar

1 vanilla pod

For the apple butter purée:

3kg apples, peeled and cored

350ml apple juice

1 tsp each of cinnamon and mixed spice

1 lemon, zest and juice

65g sugar

For the apple mousse:

400g apple purée

6 gelatine leaves

8 egg whites

80g caster sugar

240ml cream

For the caramelised milk skins:

1 litre full-cream milk

50g sugar

1 vanilla pod

For the hay ice cream:

250ml each of double cream and milk

90g caster sugar

6 egg yolks

50g fresh hay

For the salted almond crumble:

100g each of sugar and butter

50g almonds

10g flaky sea salt

For the macerated blackberries:

100g sugar

25ml Port

1 sprig of thyme

1 punnet of blackberries

Method

For the rice pudding

Mix together all the ingredients in a pan, then place the pan on the stove and cook for 20–30 minutes, stirring regularly, until the rice is soft and creamy. Discard the vanilla pod and transfer the mixture to a clean bowl, then cover it with cling film to prevent a skin from forming.

For the apple butter purée

Cook all the ingredients in a saucepan on the hob for 30 minutes, and then blend them into a purée. Pass through a fine sieve to finish.

For the apple mousse

Heat the apple purée. Soak the gelatine leaves in cold water, and then add them to the purée. Meanwhile, whisk the egg whites and sugar until soft peaks form. Whisk the cream in a separate bowl and fold it into the apple purée. Lastly, fold in the egg white mixture and the cold rice pudding, transfer into moulds and leave to chill until serving.

For the caramelised milk skins

To make the milk skins, put the milk with the sugar and vanilla pod into the oven at 180°c until a skin forms after about 15 minutes. Remove this skin carefully and allow it to dry somewhere warm.

For the hay ice cream

Mix the cream, milk and sugar in a pan and bring to the boil so the sugar dissolves. Then stir the hot mixture into the egg yolks to create custard. Add the hay and set aside to infuse for 30 minutes. Strain the liquid and place it back on the stove over a medium to high heat. Place a thermometer in the pan and bring the liquid slowly up to 76°c. Remove the mixture from the heat and allow to cool in a bowl over ice. Churn in an ice cream maker until set, and then serve.

For the salted almond crumble

Caramelise the sugar in a small saucepan over a medium heat, and then add the butter, almonds and salt. Leave to cool and then blend the mixture into a crumb.

For the macerated blackberries

Bring 100ml water to the boil with the sugar, Port and thyme in a saucepan then pour this over the blackberries. Set aside until ready to serve.

To serve

Take the rice pudding out of the mould and place it on the plate. Top with apple purée and blackberries, add a scoop of hay ice cream, place a caramelised milk skin on top and finish with a dusting of icing sugar and a sprinkle of crumble.

Sosban
COD FIVE WAYS

The motto behind this dish is 'Gran was right about cod liver oil' – not what you might expect from such a delicious recipe! Andrew's grandmother always insisted he took cod liver oil tablets as a kid and after researching the health benefits he found that she was right to, so he created a much tastier version to showcase the key ingredient.

Preparation time: 2 hours 45 minutes | Cook time: 1 hour 10 minutes | Serves: 4

Ingredients

For the cod cheeks:

150g plain flour plus extra for dusting

50g cornflour

150ml each of lager and pale ale

5g mild curry powder

Flaky sea salt and white pepper

4 cod cheeks

For the tartare sauce:

2 tbsp capers

80g cornichons, diced

250ml dill oil

2 banana shallots, minced

50g salted cod trim

1 lemon, zested and juiced

30g flat-leaf parsley, chiffonade

For the taramasalata:

50g white breadcrumbs

100ml milk

1 clove of garlic, crushed

125g smoked cod roe

2 tsp Dijon mustard

225ml grapeseed oil

3 tbsp extra-virgin olive oil

1 lemon, juiced

For the sous vide cod:

1x 250g cod fillet, skin on

For the salt and vinegar potatoes:

30g salt

30ml vinegar

300g potato

Method

For the cod cheeks

For the batter, whisk together the plain flour, cornflour, lager, ale, and curry powder until smooth, before seasoning well with sea salt and white pepper. Trim the cod cheeks, and pat dry with kitchen paper. Dust each piece of cheek in seasoned flour and then dip in the batter to coat. Gently lower each cheek into the deep-fryer and fry until it floats and the batter is golden; this should take 3–5 minutes depending on the thickness of the cheek. Set aside on kitchen paper until ready to serve.

For the tartare sauce

Dice all the ingredients, combine and then refrigerate until ready for plating.

For the taramasalata

Soak the breadcrumbs in the milk. Meanwhile, blend the garlic with the roe, mustard, a pinch of salt and three tablespoons of water in a food processor. Drain the breadcrumbs and then add them to the food processor. Blend the mixture, slowly adding the grapeseed oil a little at a time, then add the olive oil. Squeeze in the lemon juice and blend. Season to taste with white pepper and then pour the mixture into a bowl, cover with cling film and refrigerate until needed.

For the sous vide cod

Using a sharp knife, portion the cod into four 50g pieces. Poach the cod in a water bath at 50°c for 9 minutes. Remove the skins and then set the cod aside until serving.

For the cod skin

Stack the cod skins on top of each other. The stack should be around 3cm in height. Vacuum pack the skins and steam for 30 minutes. Put the steamed bag in the freezer. When frozen, remove the skins from the bag and cut the skins into 1mm slices. Dehydrate at 65°c until dry. Deep-fry the skins to make them puffy and crispy.

For the salt and vinegar potatoes

Bring 200ml water to boil and then add the salt and vinegar. Cut the potatoes with an apple corer and then blanch in the salt and vinegar water for 5 minutes until soft. Leave to air dry before blanching at 160°c for 3 minutes, then finish at 180°c for another 3 minutes until the potatoes are golden.

To serve

Place a cod cheek and a portion of sous vide cod on each plate, followed by the salt and vinegar potatoes, some tartare sauce and taramasalata. Top with crispy cod skin and serve straight away. At the restaurant, we serve this dish with pea purée and lemon gel so you get all the flavours of fish and chips on the plate.

Ticking all the
RIGHT BOXES

Burgers... but not as you know them.

Time & Beef hands the reins back to it's customers at this unique Canton eatery, where gourmet burgers built from scratch are complemented by the best coffee and cocktails the team can get their hands on. Owner and founder Steve Chambers was looking for a way to branch out from his lifelong career in hospitality and wanted to create something new in Cardiff, so decided that burgers would be the perfect vehicle for the new dining concept he had dreamt up.

The result was over 100,000 combinations and five simple steps to "the best burger you've ever had" which is Time & Beef's mission. The menu is a tick box style feast of choices for your preferred bun, patty, toppings, cheese and sauces – that's not even getting started on the light bites and sides – with space to name your burger creation as the final flourish. It's designed to be a fun and interactive dining experience that revels in all the pleasures of great food and drink as a social and creative part of your day. "We're only a small business," says Steve, "so we often get to know our customers by name and make everyone feel welcome. We offer just as many vegan and vegetarian options to make sure our burger menu is truly inclusive."

It's important to Steve that casual eating out offers quality to match the atmosphere, so his experienced chefs take over when it comes to preparing and cooking the customers' creations. Chris and Ryan are in charge of building each burger from scratch, never with frozen or pre-cooked ingredients and always with exceptional produce. Daily deliveries bring in seasonal veg and salad, as well as the fresh meat from their local butcher – with whom they worked extensively to get the cut, grind and the seasoning of their meat patties just right – and bread supplied from their award-winning artisan baker who whips up the exclusive bun options on the menu.

All this attention to detail has not only thrilled the burger fans of Cardiff, but also won Time & Beef the titles of Best Restaurant in Cardiff at the 2016 Cardiff Lifestyle Awards and Best Burger in Cardiff in a poll by Wales Online. "It's nice to be recognised for our quality and hard work," says Steve, "and it would be great to build on our success by expanding." Watch this space and prepare to get creative, Cardiff!

Time & Beef

DOUBLE BEEF BURGER WITH PORK, PEPPERS, SLAW AND CHILLI CHEESE

This particular recipe came about when our team sat together and discussed what we appreciate in a burger. We decided to use a bun unique to us in the Canton area, the seven seed potato bun and two of our 5.5oz beef patties to encase our grilled peppers and slow-cooked pork rib, topping everything off with mild cheddar and chilli flakes to bring each bite to another level!

Preparation time: 10 minutes | Cooking time: 6 hours 30 minutes | Serves: 1

Ingredients

For the slaw:

½ red cabbage, finely sliced

½ white cabbage, finely sliced

3 carrots, peeled and finely grated

150g mayonnaise

5g cracked black pepper

For the burgers:

1 whole pork rib (for the pulled pork – this will make more than you need)

½ yellow, green and red peppers

1 seven seed potato bun

2x 5.5oz coarse ground beef patties (no more than 15% fat content)

Salt and cracked black pepper

30g smoked hickory BBQ sauce

30g sliced mild cheddar

5g dried chilli flakes/crushed dried chillies

To serve:

1 chiffonade lettuce

1 beef tomato

Method

For the slaw

Place all the ingredients in a large mixing bowl and mix together until all the vegetables are coated in the mayonnaise. Season with cracked black pepper.

For the burgers

Place the pork in a medium to large gastronome tray, cover with water, place foil over the top and then cook at 165°c for 6 hours. Once cooked, drain the remaining liquid from the gastronome and shred the meat while it's hot.

Next, prepare the other fillings. Preheat a grill or griddle to 170°c and slice the peppers lengthways. Place them under the grill until soft and tender. Halve the seven seed potato bun, toast lightly, and then set aside. Place the two patties on the grill and press until just over a centimetre thick, then season with salt and cracked black pepper. Cook for 4 minutes on each side, or until they reach a minimum of 75°c, and then leave to rest.

In a separate pan, combine 150g of the pulled pork with the barbecue sauce. Leave on a low heat to warm through.

Place the burgers back on the grill and place a slice of cheese on top of each one. Sprinkle the crushed chilli over and leave on the grill to melt the cheese.

To serve

Place a nice amount of chiffonade lettuce and two slices of beef tomato onto the bottom half of the bun. Add the first beef patty and place the grilled peppers on top. Next, place the other beef patty on the stack and add the pulled pork. Finally, top it off with house slaw and gently press the bun on.

Feasts and GOOD HYWL

Wales' capital city is rich in ancient history, sporting excitement, romantic ambience, eclectic culture and (most importantly we reckon) a fantastic array of food and drink. Its coastal location has drawn influences and people from all over the world into the metropolitan hub, creating a wonderfully diverse place to live, work and visit. This diversity is reflected in the enticing mix of restaurants, producers, cafés, bars, bakeries and more across Cardiff, proving that the city's culinary offerings are just as vast and varied as its past.

From humble beginnings as a small Roman settlement to a bustling metropolitan port city, Cardiff has witnessed its fair share of milestones. The city we know and love today is the site of many firsts, from the first British news film being made there in 1896 to Captain Scott setting sail from its harbour in 1910 on his South Pole expedition. There are plenty of places to explore Cardiff's patchwork past; the museum comprises collections and displays that range from art to dinosaurs, and the Norwegian church right on the edge of the water offers an authentic look at some unusual architecture as well as Cardiff's relationship with Norwegian seafarers. Cardiff Castle, Bute Park and of course the stunning Cardiff Bay that has played such an integral role in the city's development each offer something unique to visitors and Cardiffians of all inclinations. Cardiff also has quite a few more recent claims to fame, including its connection to Roald Dahl – who was born in the city – and one of the UK's most popular and long-running sci-fi TV programmes, Doctor Who. Music buffs won't want to miss the world's oldest record store, and for eco-warriors and nature lovers the amount of green space per person across the city is hard to beat. If that wasn't enough, Cardiff also plays host to major events such as the recent UEFA Champions League and the Volvo Ocean Race.

At the beating heart of Cardiff's cultural tableau is a groaning table of gastronomic delights. The food and drink scene incorporates a wide range of influences from those passing through and moving to the well-connected city. Spanish delis, Indian restaurants, traditional Welsh fare, Danish bakery, fresh fish, vegan food from around the world, locally roasted coffee, farm-reared meat, Austrian sandwiches…the list is as long as it is mouth-watering. A number of these varied independent businesses can be found side by side in Cardiff Market. With its expansive glass roof and impressive structure, the market is a must-see and has also been the place to go for fresh produce since the 1700s. Although you'll no longer find livestock penned up outside, you will get a taste of shopping in Cardiff over the last few centuries. The city really knows how to bring its history to life and the Victorian Arcades are another great example of engaging with the past to create the future. One of the best places to find independent cafés and restaurants, the narrow lanes and architectural details within the arcades provide the perfect backdrop to an afternoon tea, a little chocolate indulgence, or even Indian street food. And we'd heartily recommend following up with a visit to the independent bars or pubs for a craft beer or three.

As one of the top five fastest-growing food and drink scenes in the UK, Cardiff places no limit on finding something to tickle your taste buds. With pop-up events and food and wine tasting tours being hosted regularly in the city, Cardiff goes out of its way to celebrate food that's new and fresh and even weird and wacky. Some of our favourite dining experiences really capture the essence of Cardiff's extensive relationship with food. Duchess of Delhi is a vibrant restaurant that resides in a building formerly owned by the Glamorgan Coal Company; this building has witnessed the area grow from a coal exportation site to an area known as 'Tiger Bay'. The aim is to serve totally authentic Indian food and shows that Asian cuisine is as much a part of Cardiff's history as Welsh food.

Continuing down the historical route, Cardiff Castle transforms into an inspiring evening venue for its Welsh Banquets. Featuring mead-tasting, entertainment which includes traditional and contemporary music sung in English and Welsh, wine and of course plenty of Welsh food, they promise to be an unforgettable example of Welsh hospitality. The Welsh Banquets are hosted in either the stone-vaulted, atmospheric 15th century undercroft or the Interpretation Centre, which offers a unique blend of contemporary slate interiors and original 4th century Roman walls with stunning views of the keep. You won't be able to resist joining in the hwyl!

If you're fond of a good spread, don't miss the Cardiff International Food and Drink Festival which fills the bay with food, drink, live music and entertainment each July. Wales' largest annual food and drink festival features stalls crammed with local produce, an extensive farmer's market, cooking demonstrations from top chefs in the area and even its own Street Food Piazza.

For year-round indulgence in the local culinary scene, Loving Welsh Food runs tasting tours designed to give people a real feel for the plethora of food on offer. The tours move around the city centre to take in the best fresh produce along with some of Cardiff's most popular landmarks. All that said, for a city with so much on offer it's almost impossible to create a shortlist of the best places to eat, drink, sightsee and generally have a great time! It's absolutely true to say that Cardiff is constantly changing and growing, so each visit offers more food, culture, history and excitement than the last and won't disappoint whether you're a first-time visitor or Cardiff born and bred.

Loving Welsh Food
GLAMORGAN SAUSAGES

Glamorgan sausages are delicious vegetarian sausages made to a very easy recipe, great for using up leftover bread and cheese. We suggest using a mature hard cheese, but you can experiment with other kinds of cheese; halloumi works very well too.

Preparation time: 15-20 minutes | Cooking time: 10 minutes | Serves: 4

Ingredients

200g white breadcrumbs

75g Welsh Cheddar

½ leek, finely chopped

½ carrot, grated

1 tbsp chopped fresh parsley

½ tsp fresh thyme leaves

Salt and pepper

2 eggs, beaten

1 tsp wholegrain mustard

Knob of butter

Method

Put three tablespoons of breadcrumbs to one side, and mix the rest with the cheese, leek, carrot, parsley, thyme and plenty of salt and pepper. Beat the eggs with the mustard. Set aside two tablespoons of this mixture, and stir the rest into the breadcrumb mixture. Divide the sausage mixture into eight and shape each portion.

Put the reserved egg and mustard mixture into a shallow bowl and spread the remaining breadcrumbs on a plate. Dip the sausages into the egg mixture and then coat with the breadcrumbs. If you are running out of the egg and mustard mixture, add a little milk.

If you have time, chill the sausages for 30 minutes before cooking. Heat the butter (you could use sunflower or vegetable oil instead) in a frying pan and fry the sausages for about 5 minutes until nicely browned. Then reduce the heat and fry for a further 3-4 minutes. Serve hot with a side of your choice.

Keeping it in THE FAMILY

Wally's Delicatessen and Kaffeehaus is a real Cardiff institution: a family business that has been in operation since 1947; a unique place to shop and eat, offering authentic products from around the world; and an oasis of calm in the city's hustle and bustle.

If you're looking for an Austrian café experience or an authentic foodstuff that you had on your holidays and can't find anywhere at home, Wally's is the place to go. The delicatessen and kaffeehaus combines a smorgasbord of delights to eat and to buy and take home, which uses passed-down knowledge, expert food importers and an eye for the unusual to provide the city with a huge international range of products and somewhere to watch the world go by.

The kaffeehaus, which sits above the delicatessen, was opened in 2011 to the tune of Austrian tradition. Everything from the décor and Bentwood style furniture to the classical music played throughout the day will transport visitors to the elegance of Vienna that Wally's is designed after. All the open sandwiches – a mainstay of café cuisine in the Germanic areas of Europe – are named after places in Austria having been developed at Wally's and the little touches like the glass of water arriving with your coffee make customers feel well looked after. The coffee menu itself is like nothing you'll have seen before in the UK either, as it uses the Germanic equivalents of the Italian names we are familiar with (milchkaffe = latte, for example!). As a showcase for the

delicatessen, the food is prepared with care, flair and passion for flavour and presentation that makes every meal – or perfect slice of sachertorte, gateau or strudel – a real treat.

Steven Salamon, the current owner, helps to educate customers with tasters and stories of his products and creations in the delicatessen and kaffeehaus, as well as responding to things they ask for. Steven joined his father in the business during its expansion in the 1970s, when the delicatessen started to include foods from all over the world, branching out from its Austrian background. It was Steven's grandfather, Ignatz, who founded the shop that would become Wally's after immigrating to Wales just before the war, having fled his home country to escape persecution. He ran a truly successful family business, handing over the shop to his sons Wally and Otto and posthumously to Steven, who saw Wally's Delicatessen and Kaffeehaus triumph in the 2017 Cardiff Family Business Award. With such longevity, innovation and respect for tradition it's hard to think of a more deserving winner!

Wally's Delicatessen and Kaffeehaus
EISENSTADT (OPEN SANDWICH)

Open sandwiches are a typical feature of the food culture in Europe, especially across Northern Europe, Germany and Austria. This open sandwich is one of the original sandwiches invented by Wally's and is named after a small village in Austria, the birthplace of the business's founder.

This open sandwich should take no more than a few minutes to prepare.

Ingredients

1 large slice of rye bread

Gooseberry and coriander chutney

1 fresh vine-ripened tomato, sliced

30g Cambozola cheese

¼ red onion, thinly sliced

A handful of rocket

A drizzle of extra-virgin olive oil

4 slices of Black Forest ham

5 slices of German onion salami

Nigella seeds, to garnish

Method

Spread a generous layer of chutney over the rye bread. Lay the tomato slices on top of the chutney. Break up the Cambozola and scatter it over the tomatoes. Combine the thinly sliced red onion with the rocket and a drizzle of the olive oil in a small mixing bowl, then pile this on top of the cheese. Drape the Black Forest ham on top of the salad and arrange the salami on top. Garnish with nigella seeds.

To serve

This open sandwich is great with a side of potato salad.

The DIRECTORY

These great businesses have supported the making of this book;
please support and enjoy them.

1861 Restaurant

Cross Ash
Near Abergavenny
Monmouthshire
NP7 8PB
Telephone:
01873 821297 / 0845 388 1861
Website: www.18-61.co.uk
*A fabulous fine dining experience,
well worth going the extra mile for.*

Anna Loka

114 Albany Road
Cardiff
CF24 3RU
Telephone: 02920 497703
Website: www.anna-loka.com
*Cardiff's first vegan café, offering an
eclectic, authentic, healthy experience
for all food lovers to enjoy delicious
meals in a relaxed environment.*

E. Ashton Fishmongers Ltd

Central Market
St Mary's St
Cardiff
CF10 1AU
Telephone: 02920 229201
Website:
www.ashtonfishmongers.co.uk
*A family-run fishmongers, great for
fresh and good quality products with
an extensive range of fish, poultry and
game.*

Brodies Coffee Co

Brodies Coffee Cabin
Gorsedd Gardens
Cathays
CF10 3NP
Telephone: 07414963591
Website:
www.brodiescoffeeco.co.uk
*A family-run, independent coffee shop
based in a beautiful park in the heart
of Cardiff.*

Brød – The Danish Bakery

126 Wyndham Crescent
Cardiff
CF11 9EG
Telephone: 02920 251822
Website:
www.thedanishbakery.co.uk
*A little taste of Denmark in the heart
of Cardiff. Take-away bakery and
cosy coffee shop full of freshly made
treats and plenty of hygge.*

The Bunch of Grapes

Ynysangharad Road
Pontypridd
Rhondda Cynon Taff
CF37 4DA
Telephone: 01443 402394
Website:
www.bunchofgrapes.org.uk
Pioneering Welsh gastropub.

Burger Theory Cardiff

92 St Marys Street
Cardiff
CF10 1DX
Website: www.burgertheory.co.uk
World cuisine in a bun brought to you by Cardiff's most creative burger chefs!

Caffi Bodlon

12 Park Road
Whitchurch
Cardiff
CF14 7BQ
Telephone: 02920 650564
Website: www.bodlon.com
An independent coffee and gift shop serving the best of Welsh ingredients based in Whitchurch.

Canna Deli

2 Pontcanna Mews
200 Kings Road
Pontcanna
Cardiff
CF11 9DF
Telephone: 07767 726902
Find us on Facebook @ cannadeliofficial
Treasure trove of unique and authentic Welsh produce, including artisan cheese from the owner's family dairy farm.

Cardiff Market

St Mary Street
Cardiff
CF10 1AU
Telephone: 02920 871214
Website:
www.cardiffcouncilproperty.com/cardiff-market
Grade II* indoor market based over two levels selling fresh produce and various goods.

Cocorico Patisserie

35 Whitchurch Road
Cardiff
CF14 3JN
Telephone: 02921 328177
Website:
www.cocoricopatisserie.co.uk
Modern patisserie creating French delicacies and serving freshly made food and drink in the café.

Curado Bar

2 Guildhall Place
Cardiff
CF10 1EB
Telephone: 02920 344336
Website: www.curadobar.com
Pintxos and ham in the heart of the city.

Ffresh

Wales Millennium Centre
Bute Place
Cardiff Bay
Cardiff
CF10 5AL
Telephone: 02920 636465
Website: www.wmc.org.uk/EatDrinkShop/ffresh
Family-friendly restaurant within the WMC, specialising in pre-theatre, traditional Welsh dining, as well as providing a wide range of cocktails and live entertainment on some evenings.

Foxy's Deli and Café

7 Royal Buildings
Victoria Road
Penarth
CF64 3ED
Telephone: 02920 251666
Website: www.foxysdeli.wales
Deli and café serving the best of Welsh produce and freshly made food alongside plenty of community spirit in Penarth.

Ginhaus Deli

1 Market Street
Llandeilo
Carmarthenshire
SA19 6AH
Telephone: 01558 823030
Website: www.ginhaus.co.uk
Deli, cafe and gin bar serving really good coffee, breakfast, lunch and plenty of gin!

Holm House Hotel and Spa

Marine Parade
Penarth
CF64 3BG
Telephone: 02920 706029
Website:
www.holmhousehotel.com
A boutique coastal hotel and spa offering the finest food and service in a beautiful location.

Restaurant James Sommerin

The Esplanade
Penarth
CF64 3AU
Telephone : 02920 706559
Website:
Jamessommerinrestaurant.co.uk
A relaxed Michelin-starred dining experience with a panoramic sea view.

Moksh

Bute Crescent
Cardiff
CF10 5AN
Telephone: 02920 498120
Website: www.moksh.co.uk
A multi award-winning Indian restaurant, delivering a sensory gastronomic experience.

Moody Sow Farm Shop

Began Road
Old St Mellons
Cardiff
CF3 6XL
Telephone: 01633 680034
Website: www.moodysow.com
Located at the Cefn Mably Farm Park, with top-quality butchery, freshly baked deli goods and the very best of Welsh and British farm produce on offer.

One Mile Bakery Cardiff

Rhiwbina
Cardiff
Telephone: 07990807709
Website: www.onemilebakery.com/cardiff
Artisan micro bakery run by Nick Macleod, offering a wide range of inspirational baking classes and also delivering handmade bread, soup and preserves by bike within a mile of Nick's kitchen.

Seren Diemwnt

48 High Street
Llandaff
CF52DZ
Telephone: 02920 564646
Website: www.seren-diemwnt.com
Restaurant with a mission to serve tantalising food at great prices that everyone will enjoy and come back for.

Sosban

North Dock
Llanelli
SA15 2LF
Telephone: 01554 270020
Website: www.sosban.wales
Innovative restaurant by Andrew Sheridan, serving seasonal dishes with bold modern flavours and exceptional ingredients.

Time & Beef

169 Cowbridge Road East
Cardiff
CF11 9AH
Telephone: 02921 158539
Website: www.timeandbeef.co.uk
Build your ideal burger from the freshest locally sourced ingredients, cooked to order for a fun and interactive dining experience.

Visit Cardiff

County Hall
Atlantic Wharf
Cardiff
CF10 4UW
Telephone: 02920 873573
Website: www.visitcardiff.com
Promoting the dynamic image of Cardiff to the world.

Wally's Delicatessen and Kaffeehaus

38-46 Royal Arcade
Cardiff
CF10 1AE
Telephone: 02920 229265
Website: www.wallysdeli.co.uk
Authenticity, variety, quality – serving gourmet fine foods from around the world.

Other titles in the 'Get Stuck In' series

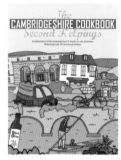

The Cambridgeshire Cook Book: Second Helpings
features Mark Abbott of Midsummer House, The Olive Grove, Elder Street Café and lots more.
978-1-910863-33-6

The Lakes & Cumbria Cook Book
features Simon Rogan's L'Enclume, Forest Side, Hawkshead Relish, L'al Churrasco and lots more.
978-1-910863-30-5

The Nottingham Cook Book: Second Helpings
features Welbeck Estate, Memsaab, Sauce Shop, 200 Degrees Coffee, Homeboys, Rustic Crust and lots more.
978-1-910863-27-5

The Devon Cook Book
sponsored by Food Drink Devon features Simon Hulstone of The Elephant, Noel Corston, Riverford Field Kitchen and much more.
978-1-910863-24-4

The South London Cook Book
features Jose Pizarro, Adam Byatt, The Alma, Piccalilli Caff, Canopy Beer, Inkspot Brewery and lots more.
978-1-910863-27-5

The Brighton & Sussex Cook Book features Steven Edwards, The Bluebird Tea Co, Isaac At, Real Patisserie, Sussex Produce Co, and lots more.
978-1-910863-22-0

The Liverpool Cook Book
features Burnt Truffle, The Art School, Fraîche, Villaggio Cucina and many more.
978-1-910863-15-2

The Bristol Cook Book
features Dean Edwards, Lido, Clifton Sausage, The Ox, and wines from Corks of Cotham plus lots more.
978-1-910863-14-5

The Leeds Cook Book
features The Boxtree, Crafthouse, Stockdales of Yorkshire and lots more.
978-1-910863-18-3

The Cotswolds Cook Book
features David Everitt-Matthias of Champignon Sauvage, Prithvi, Chef's Dozen and lots more.
978-0-9928981-9-9

The Shropshire Cook Book
features Chris Burt of The Peach Tree, Old Downton Lodge, Shrewsbury Market, CSons and lots more.
978-1-910863-32-9

The Norfolk Cook Book
features Richard Bainbridge, Morston Hall, The Duck Inn and lots more.
978-1-910863-01-5

The Derbyshire Cook Book: Second Helpings
features The Tickled Trout, The Old Hall Inn, Fredericks, The Bottle Kiln and lots more.
978-1-910863-34-3

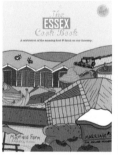

The Essex Cook Book features Thomas Leatherbarrow, The Anchor Riverside, Great Garnetts, Deersbrook Farm, Mayfield Bakery and lots more.
978-1-910863-25-1

The Cheshire Cook Book
features Simon Radley of The Chester Grosvenor, The Chef's Table, Great North Pie Co., Harthill Cookery School and lots more.
978-1-910863-07-7

All books in this series are available from Waterstones, Amazon and independent bookshops.

FIND OUT MORE ABOUT US AT WWW.MEZEPUBLISHING.CO.UK